Second
Edition

LEADING PROJECT TEAMS

Second
Edition

LEADING PROJECT TEAMS

The Basics of Project Management and Team Leadership

Anthony T. Cobb
Virginia Tech

SAGE

Los Angeles | London | New Delhi
Singapore | Washington DC

Los Angeles | London | New Delh
Singapore | Washington DC

FOR INFORMATION:

SAGE Publications, Inc.
2455 Teller Road
Thousand Oaks, California 91320
E-mail: order@sagepub.com

SAGE Publications Ltd.
1 Oliver's Yard
55 City Road
London EC1Y 1SP
United Kingdom

SAGE Publications India Pvt. Ltd.
B 1/I 1 Mohan Cooperative Industrial Area
Mathura Road, New Delhi 110 044
India

SAGE Publications Asia-Pacific Pte. Ltd.
33 Pekin Street #02-01
Far East Square
Singapore 048763

Senior Executive Editor: Lisa Cuevas Shaw
Senior Editorial Assistant: MaryAnn Vail
Production Editor: Libby Larson
Permissions Editor: Karen Ehrmann
Copy Editor: Matthew Adams
Typesetter: C&M Digitals (P) Ltd.
Proofreader: Susan Schon
Indexer: Wendy Allex
Cover Designer: Candice Harman
Marketing Manager: Helen Salmon

Printed in the United States of America.

Library of Congress Cataloging-in-Publication Data

Cobb, Anthony T.

Leading project teams: the basics of project management and team leadership/Anthony T. Cobb.—2nd ed.

p. cm.
Rev. ed. of: Leading project teams: an introduction to the basics of project management and project team leadership. c2006.

Includes bibliographical references and index.

ISBN 978-1-4129-9170-4 (pbk.)

1. Project management. 2. Teams in the workplace. I. Title.

HD69.P75C616 2012 658.4'092—dc22
2010051832

This book is printed on acid-free paper.

11 12 13 14 15 10 9 8 7 6 5 4 3 2 1

Brief Contents

Detailed Contents

1

Introduction

I nterest in and demand for project management has increased a great deal over the past 20 years. This increase in interest and demand can be seen in a number of ways. One way is in the number of books oriented to project management, which now number in the thousands. Another is in the growth of training programs offered in project management, which are now widely available and also number in the thousands.[1] Still a third way is in college recruiting. Recruiters often develop much more interest in students when they mention their project management training or their experience in leading project teams. Perhaps most indicative of interest in project management is the results one gets from simply "Googling" project management.

Part of this increase in demand is due to growth in what can be called "traditional" project work. Most of the early work in project management was done by engineers working for large "performing" companies that conducted large-scale projects for outside clients.[2] Working on projects like high-rise construction or large weapon systems, these professionals developed most of the project management tools we now use. Certainly, demand for these kinds of projects has increased over the years.

Interest in project management, however, has grown in a number of other areas as well. One of these areas is new product development. Product life cycles have shrunk a great deal because organizations have turned to using new product development as a competitive strategy. To remain competitive, organizations have to constantly update and remodel what they offer their customers. Companies have found that bringing new products to market is best managed in a project environment using cross-functional project teams.

Another area of growth is in the demand for new organizational processes. Organizations not only have to constantly develop new products to remain competitive, but they have to constantly develop themselves as well. From quality circles to "Tiger Teams," organizations have looked to project teams to reinvent and reengineer themselves to attain ever-increasing levels of quality and efficiency.

These kinds of challenges have produced what might be called a "project mindset." Whenever something of significance needs to be done—a problem solved or an opportunity seized—higher management assembles project teams to do the work. Whether the projects are making process improvements, starting new ventures, developing new client services, finding and opening new market niches, or even running political campaigns, leaders have come to value project management tools and skills in planning and conducting them.

With this broadening of project work, the composition of project teams has also changed. Although many are still composed of builders or engineers, most are not. Members come from all walks of life and from all professions. Project teams are assembled in laboratories, universities, government offices, school districts, on the shop floor, and in the executive suite, to name just a few project "work sites."

The level of skills required for these project teams has also changed. Although the full range of skills used by professional project engineers is always useful, most of the need is for more entry-level project skills. Smaller projects depend less on sophisticated tools to do such tasks as cost or risk analysis and depend much more on tools needed to organize projects, clarify deliverables, work with stakeholders, and manage and lead project teams.

This book is written to help convey entry-level project tools and skills for the newcomer to project management. It is designed so it can be used as a supplemental text in courses dedicated to topics other than project management. In these kinds of venues, its aims are twofold. First, it aims to help student teams become more effective at doing course projects by learning project management techniques and applying them to their work. Teams are simply more effective and learn more when they have the skills to do the course's projects well. Second, it aims to help prepare students to enter the kind of "project life" that has come to dominate so much of modern organizational work. From whatever area of study students emerge, recruiters see project training and experience as value added, and this gives the student a comparative advantage over those who have not benefited from such training.

This book, then, is designed to be of help in a wide range of professional programs. This includes, of course, undergraduate and MBA-level business courses such as business strategy, entrepreneurship, organizational behavior, information systems, project management, and operations management, among others. It was also written, however, to serve project management needs in a wider range of curricula including education, health care, sciences, information technology, engineering, political science, and other programs whose students will someday be called on to lead project work in their field. Since its first publication, it has been used in a variety of consulting and training venues as well.

In the remainder of this chapter, we examine some of the fundamental notions of what characterizes projects and what makes them unique. We then turn our attention to how the basic tools of project management are addressed in this book as well as essential elements of successful project leadership.

PROJECT FUNDAMENTALS

DEFINING CHARACTERISTICS OF PROJECTS

The Project Management Institute defines a **project** as a temporary endeavor undertaken to create a unique product, service, or result.[3] The two defining characteristics of projects, then, are that they are unique and temporary.

Projects Are Unique

Projects are unique in terms of the outcomes they produce. Just how unique they are, however, can vary a great deal. At one extreme, we might find the development of new weapons systems. They may require yet-to-be-developed composites for armor, space-age munitions, cutting-edge guidance systems, and the like. Most projects, however, produce products and services far less exotic. Custom-built homes, for example, are unique from one another but similar in other respects: basics of foundations, wiring, plumbing, and the like. When a company opens a new market area, it is likely producing a unique outcome, although the company may have opened many others in the past—each new one is likely different in some significant way from all the others. Although these projects may not present the design challenges of a new weapons system, those who lead them know how challenging they are.

This leads us to another aspect of what makes projects unique. They are unique in terms of how they are conducted. They are unique in terms of their staffing, their stakeholders, the resources used, when things have to be done, how work is to be coordinated, and a host of other operational aspects.

It is because organizations face these kinds of challenges on an almost daily basis that project management tools and skills have become so much in demand. There is little doubt that these tools and skills can help with these kinds of projects. How they are used to plan and control a project, however, is always a problem-solving process, and each new project has to be handcrafted.

Projects Are Temporary

Projects are also temporary endeavors. They have a life cycle that fundamentally affects their structure, dynamics, and operations and, as a result, their management. Project life cycles have been described in a number of ways, but we will focus on five stages: initiation, planning, launch, execution, and closing.[4] **Project initiation** is the stage in which a project's key stakeholders first come together to define the broad outlines of a project. A key objective of this stage is to come to a common understanding of what the project is supposed to produce and estimate what it will take to do so. Given this understanding and these estimates, another key objective is to decide whether to move forward with the project.

In organizations dedicated to project work, the initiation phase results in an assessment of whether a project fits with the organization's profit goals or business model. We examine it here in a more general way—to make sure significant stakeholders are on board before moving too far down the road.

The **project planning** stage emerges once a decision is made to move forward. Here, more detailed planning is done to "nail down" a wide range of project specifics, including the precise tasks required to produce the project's products and services, more precise estimates of resource needs and their costs, and the time required to perform project work. In addition, how project tasks will be arranged across the project's life cycle will be determined and mapped onto a project schedule. These come together in a project plan—a blueprint—of what the project will look like, and the plan is used in the actual conduct of the project. This plan, too, needs to be approved by significant stakeholders before major project work actually begins.

The **project launch** is done once the planning is complete and initial resources are committed. Beginning the actual work on a project is a critical juncture in any project's life and demands a great deal of leader attention. Not the least of this attention is aimed at assembling the right project team, structuring the team so that it can reach its potential, and correctly initiating its project work.

The major objective of the **project execution** stage—the stage in which tasks are delegated to team members and most of the project's work is done—is to keep the project on track once it has been launched. Working with the project team, leaders need to monitor and control the pace of project work, its costs, and performance quality. Working with external stakeholders, leaders need to maintain project support; ensure flow of project resources; and minimize but adapt to project pressures, disruptions, and changes.

Finally, in the **project closing** phase, final products, services, and other project outcomes are delivered to the client. Project ties to the performing or host organization are retired, and the project team itself disbands. Each of these activities requires proper managerial and leadership attention.

PROJECT PARAMETERS

There are three major parameters to every project: project scope, costs, and time. *Project scope* refers to the sum total of all work to be done to produce the project's deliverables—the products and services to be delivered to the customer. *Costs* are the sum total of project costs to do the project's work. Finally, *time* is the amount of time given to complete the project.

These parameters are closely linked. If the project's scope of work changes to accommodate a change in deliverables, for example, costs and time are affected. If a project is given more time, on the other hand, work might consume fewer resources, resulting in lower cost. Costs generally increase, however, when the time given to do the project is shortened. Close attention needs to be given to each of these areas from the very beginning of a project through its execution.

DIMENSIONS OF PROJECT LEADERSHIP

Although there are many dimensions of leadership, the literature has traditionally focused on two: the task and social-psychological dimensions. Traditional project management attends well to the task side of project leadership. Project tools help leaders do a variety of task work, including clarifying the project's mission and objectives; planning, organizing, and structuring project work; coordinating the flow of resources and task outputs; and controlling the operational side of project work.

The social-psychological dimension of leadership focuses on how leaders operate in the social context and in one-on-one relationships that surround and support task work. Much of this literature focuses on leader-subordinate relationships and is relevant to working with the project team. Among other things, leaders need to staff, develop, motivate, and ensure commitment from their project teams.

Project leaders must also attend to the broader social context in which their projects reside. Leaders need to identify and work with their key project stakeholders, taking into account their interests and needs. Project leaders bridge the gap between their teams and the project's other stakeholders. Being the key liaison between these two worlds, leaders must be able to communicate effectively with both team members and stakeholders. They must negotiate agreement between and among them, solve personal and political as well as technical problems, and maintain support and commitment to the project from all parties, to name just a few job responsibilities. Faced with challenges such as these, it is not surprising that many project leaders wish all they had to worry about was the task side of projects, no matter how complicated and complex they may be.

This book is oriented to these kinds of issues. In the first part, the task side of project leadership is given primary attention. Project management tools are presented and discussed in terms of how they are used by project leaders. In the second part of the book, leadership issues come to the fore-front. We focus on the team, the project's stakeholders, and the leader him-self or herself. A final chapter is devoted to project reports.

OVERVIEW OF BOOK

This book is divided into two major sections. The first focuses on tools lead-ers use in project initiation and planning. The second section focuses on the human resources of project leadership and includes attention to writing up project reports.

CHAPTERS 2–5: FUNDAMENTALS OF PROJECT INITIATION AND PLANNING

Chapters 2 through 5 are devoted to project initiation and planning. Although technical issues receive the most attention, managerial and leader-ship issues are also discussed. The purpose of this section is to help the reader develop an entry-level understanding of these project management tools and how project leaders use them.

Chapter 2: Determining the Direction and Initial Specifications of a Project

This chapter is designed to help new project leaders sort out what to do when they are first approached about a project and the steps they need to take to initiate it. The objective of project initiation is to determine the basic parameters of a project so stakeholders can make decisions about whether to move ahead with it.

We begin by discussing the project's basic mission statement and how to identify those who have an important stake in the project. Next, we exam-ine how to refine the project's broad mission into concrete deliverables—the products, services, and other outcomes the project is responsible for pro-ducing. Then, we discuss developing good early estimates of a project's resource, cost, and time requirements. Before a project moves too far for-ward, relevant stakeholders need a good estimate of these requirements and must agree to them. Finally, we discuss the need to develop a project charter that lays out the important parameters of the project so all relevant stake-holders can review and sign off on it. We wrap by outlining some of the essential elements of the project's plan—the blueprint of the project that will be developed over the next few chapters.

Chapter 3: The Work Breakdown Structure

The operational foundation of any project is the scope of work needed to produce its deliverables. The work breakdown structure helps create that foundation by detailing all the tasks needed in a project. This chapter reviews what work breakdown structures are; how they are developed; and how they are used in project planning, organization, and control.

We examine first what a work breakdown structure is and the various roles it plays in project planning and control. We go on to discuss how work breakdown structures are developed, focusing on both core and support tasks in the project. Finally, we discuss how work breakdown structures are used to estimate project resources, timelines, and costs. We attend as well to how work breakdown structures can be used to develop the project's organizational structure.

Chapter 4: Project Scheduling

Project schedules arrange when project tasks are to be done across the project's life cycle. The project schedule is a principal managerial tool used to organize, coordinate, and control project work.

First, we review three common scheduling tools and how they are used. Next, we discuss the basic components of any project schedule and their uses. We then focus on the Gantt or bar chart and discuss how to construct it. Finally, we discuss the various ways project leaders can use schedules to plan, organize, and control a project.

Chapter 5: Managing Project Risk

Because projects produce new and unique products and have so many stakeholders, they carry with them a great deal of risk. Managing that risk is an important task for any project leader. This chapter presents some of the principal ideas behind risk management in project planning and execution.

First, we examine the principal sources of risk in project work: risk from the project itself, from the host organization, from producing deliverables, and from the larger project environment. Next, we discuss how risk is assessed using both qualitative and quantitative methods. We then review four common methods of dealing with risk: accepting it, avoiding it, reducing it, and transferring the risk to others. Finally, we discuss how a risk management plan is developed and used in project execution.

Chapters 6–8: Fundamentals of Project Leadership

Project leadership requires working effectively with two groups of project participants: the project team and external project stakeholders. In Chapter 6, we examine how best to construct and develop project teams to do project work. In Chapter 7, we identify who stakeholders are, their differing interests, and some ways to work with them. Chapter 8 focuses specifically on project leadership.

Chapter 6: Developing Project Teams

Project teams are the key resource leaders use in any project. This chapter is designed to help project leaders understand how teams are best constructed and developed. We cover first what a team is and what constitutes team success. We then turn attention to those elements of a team's structure that can help or hinder its success. Team factors covered include team size, composition, governance, identity, interactions, and a common team mindset. These factors need to be given attention in the construction of a team and its development.

We end by discussing the developmental stages groups go through on their way to becoming truly effective teams: forming, storming, norming, performing, and adjourning. We discuss the characteristics of each stage and, importantly, what teams need from their leaders to be effective and to progress further in their development.

Chapter 7: The Project Team's Environment

Projects operate in an environment of stakeholders who will influence and likely determine project success. Leaders need to work in this environment to make sure the project gets the support and resources it needs to complete its work. This chapter identifies the characteristics and needs of a project's principal stakeholders and how to work effectively in the project's stakeholder network.

We begin by identifying some of the more important project stakeholders and provide suggestions about how best to work with them. Project leaders play a key liaison role in tying these stakeholders together and to the project. Properly used, this liaison role can provide the leader with the social capital he or she needs to acquire critical project resources and support. We examine social networks and the social capital that comes from them in this chapter, as well as how project leaders can develop and use them.

Chapter 8: Leading Project Teams

Project leaders are expected to play a number of roles in any project. We review those roles and the expectations that come with them, and we offer suggestions about how best to address those expectations. Projects need different things from their leaders at different stages in their life cycle. We address those needs and how to meet them during project initiation and planning, project launch, execution, and, finally, project closing. Finally, we focus on how project leaders can help individual project members develop within the project to add value to it.

CHAPTER 9: WRITING PROJECT REPORTS

Projects often require a number of reports to be produced at various times in their life cycles. We focus on the final, formal project report to address issues important to any project report. Writing effective reports requires knowledge of who will read them and what they are looking for in project reports. We begin by identifying some of the more important readers of project reports and how best to address their needs. We then turn our attention to the report itself. Our approach is to walk through the final project report and discuss how different sections of the report should be written. We start with the front end, addressing such elements as the cover page, the table of contents, and, most important, the executive summary. We then turn attention to the body of the report, covering introductions, major sections and subsections, conclusions and recommendations, and references. We finish with a discussion of supporting appendices. At each juncture, we discuss basic elements of the section and how to address the needs of different readers.

SUMMARY

Interest in project management has increased dramatically over the past 20 years. Much of this increase can be attributed to increased demand for more traditional projects conducted by larger construction and engineering firms. Most of the increase, however, has come from smaller scale projects aimed at different missions, staffed by a wider range of project personnel, and often conducted by organizations for themselves. Although sophisticated project management skills and tools are always useful, these kinds of smaller projects have increased the demand for what might be called a more entry-level skill set. This book is addressed to those skills and tools.

Projects are temporary endeavors undertaken to create unique products, services, or other outcomes. Projects are unique not only in the outcomes they produce but in the design and operation of the projects themselves. Each project is, to some extent, handcrafted, and leaders need to learn the basic tools to do the work anew with each new project. Projects are also temporary endeavors that have a life cycle that deeply affects project operations and leadership requirements. The stages of a project can be broken out into initiation, planning, launch, execution, and closing. Each stage has its own objectives and needs to which leaders must attend.

All projects have three basic parameters: project scope, cost, and time. Project scope is the sum total of tasks needed to produce the products and services of a project—its deliverables. The costs of a project are all related costs that are expended in doing project work. Time is the time given to the project to complete its work. These three parameters are connected so that increases or decreases in one will affect one or more of the others.

Two basic dimensions of leadership are explored in this book: the task and social-psychological sides of leadership. The task dimension focuses on what is needed to get the task done. Project management tools and techniques go a long way toward addressing these needs. The first part of this book focuses on this aspect of project leadership: project direction and specification, the work breakdown structure, and project schedules.

The social-psychological dimension focuses on how leaders operate in the broader social and personal context of the project. The second part of this book deals with addressing these needs: constructing and developing teams, identifying and dealing with project stakeholders, exploring the leadership role, and communicating with stakeholders through project reports.

ENDNOTES

1. The reader is invited to do a Google search on "training project management" to see current offerings.

2. Those who pay for getting project work done are called by various names. The term *client* is often used in the consulting industry. *Customer* is used most often by organizations that do work for the federal government and by the Project Management Institute. The terms *client* and *customer* are used interchangeably here. The label of *end user* will be used to specify those who will actually use the output of a project. Often that is the client or customer paying for the project, but it need not be. Although the military procures fighter aircraft, for example, the pilots and maintenance crews are the end users.

3. The Project Management Institute. (2008). *A guide to the project management body of knowledge*. Newtown Square, PA: Author.

4. These labels are taken in large part from what the Project Management Institute (2008) characterized as the basic processes that occur in different project phases: initiating, planning, executing, monitoring and controlling, and closing. Here, *executing* refers to the actual conduct of the project, which includes monitoring and controlling processes. *Launch* is added to give special focus to the initial process of assembling resources and kicking off the project. This short but critical stage requires the undivided attention of project leaders.

KEY TERMS

Project: a temporary endeavor undertaken to create a unique product, service, or result.

Project Closing: the stage in which final products, services, and other project outcomes are delivered to the client.

Project Execution: the stage in which tasks are delegated to team members and most of the project's work is done.

Project Initiation: the stage in which a project's key stakeholders first come together to define the broad outlines of a project.

Project Launch: the stage in which actual work on the project is begun.

Project Planning: the stage in which more detailed planning is done to establish a wide range of project specifics, ending with the creation of a project schedule and plan.

2

Determining the Direction
and Initial Specifications
of a Project

INTRODUCTION

THE BALTIMORE PROJECT

John had no idea what was coming when he picked up his phone early one Monday morning at the corporate offices of Acme Auto Supply. Acme Auto is a midsized company that grossed more than $500 million in revenues last year and is gaining a reputation on Wall Street as an aggressive and growing company.

"Hey, John, you got a minute? I'd like to chat with you about a job I have in mind." It was Carol Byrnes, the director of John's division. Ten minutes later, John was getting comfortable in Carol's office and wondering what was on her mind. "You know, John, we are opening our new store in Baltimore come June 15th." "Yes, Ms. Byrnes, I've heard it's going to be some event!" "Well, that's right," Carol said. "That's why I called you. It's important that we open the store well because it is our first entry in this new market area.

In fact, we want this opening to exceed any of our others. The brass is looking to see how well the store starts out to determine the extent and pace of rolling out all our other planned stores in the Northeast corridor." "Guess that makes sense," John replied, trying to figure out why Carol was telling him all this.

"Well, John, I'd like you to take on the opening. I've talked to Ralph [John's boss] and a few other division folks, and we all are agreed you can handle this project. It means a lot to the organization and a lot to us in the division. If all goes well, it can mean a lot to you as well. Ralph can clear your plate of the Carlisle account, and we can give you Tom and, maybe, Alice to help. Can you run with this?"

What else could he say? "Sure, I'd love the opportunity." "Great!" Carol replied. "You'll need to draw up some plans for the 'Baltimore Project,' including a preliminary budget, and I'll want to review them, but let's have an initial talk tomorrow to see what you have come up with by then." Carol looked at her calendar. "Let's see, hmm, how about 3:00 tomorrow for an initial run through? I've got a half-hour slot open." "I'll see you at your office at 3:00, then," John replied, already beginning to get nervous about a high-visibility project dumped in his lap that he knew little to nothing about and that was only 6 weeks away from completion.

CHAPTER OVERVIEW

New projects can provoke more than a little anxiety even for those who deal with them often. This particular one is more than likely to do so. It is a high-visibility project; John has never opened a store before; and he has no idea how to get started. On top of it all, John wants to look good tomorrow for his meeting with Ms. Byrnes.

When any client brings a project to a project leader, the leader needs to develop an initial overview plan of the project: what the project is trying to achieve; who the important stakeholders are; and rough estimates of the work, cost, time, and other requirements of the project. Once done, the leader needs to review the project's initial plan with the key stakeholders involved and get their commitment to it. Preparing for this task is John's job for his next meeting with Carol. The steps John needs to take are the subject of this chapter.

We begin by examining the project's mission and some of the stakeholders who have an interest in it. We then focus attention on the project's more concrete objectives and its deliverables. Next, we address some of the other components of any project—its scope, resource, time, and cost estimates. These are brought together in the project's charter—the initial overview of a project's plan to be approved by the leader's superiors. We wrap things up by pointing out the other elements needed in a full project plan once the project charter is approved.

THE PROJECT'S MISSION STATEMENT

All projects have a mission. That mission is to help address some need, solve some problem, or seize some opportunity for a client. Constructing a formal mission statement helps leaders to understand and clarify the broader aims of a project, and mission statements themselves play a number of useful roles in it. Writing a mission statement is the first step project leaders need to take.

As a project leader begins to organize the project around its mission, it is important as well to identify the important stakeholders of the project. Who those stakeholders are, and what interests they have in the project, are important determinates of any project's success or failure.

What Is a Project Mission Statement and What Role Does It Play?

A **mission statement** states the purpose of a project—its general direction and aims. In a few sentences or paragraphs, it states what the project and its sponsoring clients are trying to achieve. Mission statements play a number of roles in a project, but two are very important. The first is that a mission statement helps establish and maintain the project's overall direction. The second is that it can help establish "common ground" among a project's stakeholders.

Provides Project Direction

Many people play different roles in a project and make a variety of contributions to it. All those roles and contributions are supposed to fit together in some way to produce what the project is expected to deliver. Mission statements help tie all these contributions together. In managerial terms, a mission statement helps provide unity of purpose and unity of effort in the project. It does so by clarifying the project's goals and requirements.

When a project team is first assembled, for example, the mission statement provides a common orientation to the project and its direction. As work is broken down and assigned, members can see how their efforts contribute to the project's mission as a whole. As a project moves forward, project members quite often work at different locations and narrow their project focus to their own particular jobs. The project's mission statement can help team members make sure their individual efforts will contribute to the team's goals for the entire project.

In a similar manner, those outside the project team can also assess their contributions in terms of the project's mission. Mission statements provide suppliers, consultants, regulators, and other external contributors with a common idea of the aims of a project and their role in it.

Establishes Common Ground

Mission statements that are designed with the principal stakeholders' advice and consent become a declaration of the stakeholders' common aim. As such, they provide common ground for those stakeholders' interests. That common ground can be used throughout the project to keep stakeholder ties strong, especially when unforeseen events arise and call for project changes. In these cases, the interests of different stakeholders may come into conflict, but mission statements help the principal stakeholders to keep their "eyes on the prize"—the project's ultimate purpose. During such times, the broader aims of a mission statement can provide a common "venue" where stakeholders can negotiate in good faith.

STAKEHOLDERS IN THE PROJECT'S MISSION

Any project will have a number of **stakeholders**—those who have an interest in the mission of a project or how it will be achieved and who can deeply affect it in some way. Success or failure of a project often turns on how well project leaders identify and work with these critical project stakeholders.

Important stakeholders in any project include the clients of the project and the host or performing organization in which the project is being done. The project team is an important stakeholder, as are the end users and various resource suppliers.

The Client

The project's **client** or customer[1] is the reason a project exists. It is the person or organization for whom the project is being conducted and who is paying for it. Every project is designed to address some need brought by a client, and the client is the ultimate source of funding and resources for the project. Clients' interests lie in having their needs met as much as possible, as quickly as possible, and, generally, for as low a price as possible.

The Host Organization

The performing or **host organization**[2] is the organization in which the project is conducted. The traditional model is that clients come to an organization to serve their needs. The organization, in turn, assembles project teams to do so. The interests of host organizations include making a profit from the endeavor and keeping the project and other parts of the organization running smoothly.

Organizations quite often undertake projects for their own purposes. Developing a new car model, for example, is a rather large project conducted periodically by automobile companies. Opening new markets (like John is helping to do), developing new products and services, conducting comprehensive studies of some aspect of an organization, and designing and leading organizational change are other common examples of projects conducted by organizations for their own benefit.[3] When organizations embark on such endeavors, project leaders are dealing with a stakeholder who is a client as well as the host organization and must address both sets of stakeholder needs at the same time.

The Project Team

The **project team**—the group of people who actually carry out project activities—is a critical stakeholder of any project, and the project leader will do well to look out for its interests even before it is assembled. Although project teams have many interests, an overriding one is simply to be able to do the project given the time and cost constraints and the products and services to be delivered. Other key interests are to have a smoothly running project with minimum disruption from changes and having the resources to do the job when they are needed.

End Users

End users are those ultimately intended to use or benefit from a project. Their interests focus on the utility of what is produced for them. The end users of the Baltimore Project, for example, are the intended customers of the Baltimore store. The gala opening will be successful only to the extent that potential customers are attracted to it. This, in turn, affects decisions about what kinds of advertising to use and the promotional incentives offered.

Suppliers

Projects often need **suppliers** to deliver the products and services that the team itself cannot supply. Many of these are provided by suppliers outside the host organization also called vendors, sellers, and subcontractors. The primary interest of outside suppliers is to increase their revenues by servicing the project. Often, their interests focus more on revenues than on other issues important to the project. Projects may also have internal suppliers within the host organization, however, who are called upon to help supply information, personnel, space, equipment, and the like. Quite often, the costs of these resources are not reimbursed. As one might imagine, this can set up a supplier-project relationship far different from one in which an outside supplier is paid for products and services. At the very least, project leaders need to be sensitive to the fact that supplies provided to the project often come at a cost to the internal supplier.

Dealing With Stakeholders

We have identified a number of stakeholder categories and will explore them and others much more in Chapter 7 as well as how best to work with them. For now, however, project leaders should remember that when they are dealing with stakeholders, they need to carefully consider their interests and concerns. In addition, leaders need to be aware of who are the key stakeholders for their projects. **Key stakeholders** are those who have the power and authority to make important decisions about the conduct and outcomes of the project. Although all stakeholders should command attention and respect, key stakeholders require extra time and attention.

As project leaders work through their mission statements and progress through the scoping of a project, they need to keep the principal stakeholders of the project in mind. These stakeholders often have conflicting interests that must be reconciled for the project to be a success. Although always a challenge, addressing those interests is far easier to do earlier in the project than later.

THE BALTIMORE PROJECT

It should not take John long to develop a workable mission statement for his project. A thoughtful review of those affected by the project will also point to its principal stakeholders. As a beginning, John's mission statement might state,

> The Baltimore opening is to be a gala event designed to attract Acme's principal customer base to view the products and services offered by the Baltimore store. The event will occur on or about June 15th.[4]

The stakeholders of this project include Ms. Byrnes and "the brass" in the host organization, who also play the role of clients of the project. Ralph,

John's immediate supervisor, is an important stakeholder as well. Other stakeholders include the manager of the Baltimore store and the end users the event is supposed to attract: the potential retail and business customers of the store. The project team includes John as project leader and both Tom and Alice as project members who were "volunteered" by Ms. Byrnes. Someone at the Baltimore store might also be recruited to play a role on the project team.

As the project moves forward, vendors will be added to the stakeholder list who will supply advertising for the opening (e.g., newspapers, radio) and supplies for the store itself as the site for the opening's events (e.g., caterers, performers, and store vendors who will demonstrate their products to store customers).

John has laid out the general direction of the project and identified some of its key stakeholders. John needs to turn his attention now to the more specific objectives of the project and the specific products and services his project will provide to achieve those objectives—its deliverables.

THE PROJECT'S OBJECTIVES AND DELIVERABLES

A few years ago, I was teaching a master's in business administration class about the basics of project management when an interesting event occurred. Project teams were presenting project proposals to other teams, who were acting in the role of clients. The project leader of one team finished presenting her team's proposal when one of the more experienced students began questioning her quite aggressively. "Would the project turn in a quality product, at cost, on schedule?" demanded the student/client. "Of course!" responded the project lead. "Will you guarantee satisfaction with the product?" After thinking for a moment, the project leader said, "Of course." At that point, the client turned to me and simply smiled—he had forced the project leader into an impossible position. No matter what was produced, it need not be "satisfactory" in the eyes of the client. The client could now make additional demands throughout the project on the grounds that it was not proceeding in a "satisfactory" manner.

At least two important lessons were learned that day. First, stakeholders have interests of their own that they pursue—sometimes very aggressively. Even if a stakeholder is not adversarial, honest disagreements can arise, and they usually come up "down the road" in projects, when things are tough to change. The second lesson was that although client satisfaction is always paramount, just what *will* satisfy a client should be hammered out *before* the project gets under way. "Of course," the project lead might have replied, "and we will work very closely with you in the planning process to specify what exactly will satisfy your needs before we begin the project."

Every project leader is faced with this same problem: What exactly can be done to satisfy the client—and can it be done on schedule and on budget? Once the general direction is given by the mission statement, the project's more specific objectives and deliverables need to be developed to help answer these questions.

WHAT ARE PROJECT OBJECTIVES AND DELIVERABLES?

Project objectives are those outcomes a project needs to achieve to fulfill its mission. John's project, for example, may well have a number of project objectives. One objective might focus on the effects of the event itself—what kinds of customers show up and how many. Another might focus on the advertising designed to get them to show up—who will it reach?

The project's **deliverables** are the specific products and services produced to achieve those objectives. Project deliverables include interim as well as final deliverables. Final deliverables include the products and services the project is to ultimately provide the client. Once these deliverables are provided, the project's mission is complete—the job is done. For example, John is likely to deliver some kind of advertising campaign for the project along with other final deliverables. Interim deliverables are products and services that support the development of final deliverables. For example, Ms. Byrnes might want John to produce reports on the effectiveness and costs of the various ways advertising can be done prior to her approval.[5]

ROLES PLAYED BY PROJECT'S OBJECTIVES AND DELIVERABLES

Project objectives and deliverables play a variety of roles in a project. One is that they help clients define their goals in concrete terms. Another is that they provide the project team with specific outcomes to achieve. Still a third role is that they force stakeholders to make hard choices and trade-offs as they pursue their interests.

Helping Clients Define Their Goals

When clients first present their projects—their needs, problems, goals, and ideas—they are often ambiguous at best. Developing a mission statement is an important first step in clarifying their aims. The process of developing project objectives and their deliverables moves the project forward another important step. It helps clients think through exactly what will address their needs given their resource and time constraints. Helping clients define their goals in concrete, "doable" terms is one of the most important services project leaders can provide.[6]

Providing Team Direction

Project objectives and deliverables also play an important role for the project team. Once specified, they can be translated into specific tasks needed to achieve them. Project teams can then use these tasks to direct individual and team efforts. Specificity is the key here, and the best objectives are **SMART**. They are Specific and Measurable. They are also Actionable—suggestive of the actions needed to achieve them—and Realistic—achievable even if challenging. Finally, they are Time-specific; they have a time frame within which they are to be achieved.[7]

Securing Stakeholder Agreement

Developing a project's objectives and deliverables also forces stakeholders to confront and work through their different interests. Projects often have a number of clients, for example, and each can have his or her own desires and interests. In John's project, Ms. Byrnes and the store manager are clients who are likely to have different desires and needs. In addition, clients will have different interests than host organizations, and project teams will have their own concerns as well. Developing a common set of project objectives and deliverables sets up a process by which different stakeholders must negotiate their interests to arrive at a specific set of concrete project outcomes. It also allows project teams and stakeholders to confront the hard choices earlier in the project rather than later, when adjustments are more difficult or impossible to make.[8]

THE BALTIMORE PROJECT

As stated earlier, John's project calls for at least two sets of project objectives. The first focuses on what the grand opening is trying to achieve—getting potential customers to show up for the opening. The second focuses on promotion—how to get them there. Acme Auto Supply primarily sells to two kinds of customers—to the retail "do-it-yourself" market and to professional auto mechanics. How many of each will actually show up during the grand opening would be a measure of the first project objective. The second project objective regarding promotion might set advertising targets to reach 80% of the general population within a 10-mile radius of the store and reach 99% of all auto repair shops within a 15-mile radius. The kinds of advertising and promotions used might differ, as well, between these two kinds of customers.

Given these objectives, project deliverables need to be developed to target those customers. Specific advertising and promotional incentives need to be designed, for example, that would interest them. Advertising by radio, local television, print media, and direct mailings are all possible deliverables that need to be considered for getting the message out.

Importantly, John will need to work closely with the store manager in this project. The store manager is a principal stakeholder with whom John will need to clarify promotional and other needs about the opening event itself (e.g., where it is to be held and whether refreshments and entertainment are to be provided). An example of John's project mission, some project objectives, and related, possible deliverables is given in Table 2.1.

Table 2.1   Illustration of John's Mission Statement, a Project Objective, and Its Deliverables

- **Project mission:** The mission of this project is to develop and stage the opening of the new Baltimore store. The opening is to be a gala event designed to attract Acme's principal customer base to view the products and services offered by the store. The event will occur on or about June 15th.
- **Project objectives:** [9]
- **Promotion:** The project's advertising will reach at least 80% of the general population within a 10-mile radius of the store, notifying them of the store's opening, the opening events, and any other promotional offerings. The project will also notify 99% of all auto repair shops within a 15-mile radius of the store about the store's opening, opening events of special interest to them, special services the store will offer to professional mechanics, and any special promotional offers targeting them.
- **Customers attending:** The opening events aim to attract at least 100 potential retail customers and representatives from at least 50% of auto repair shops within a 15-mile radius.
- **Project deliverables:** Advertising
- **General population:** Newspaper copy will advertise the opening of the store every day for a week prior to its opening. The copy will include a description of the event and coupons for promotional items (to be determined by store manager). Radio spots will be given about the store, its grand opening, and sale items (to be determined by store manager) on three of the area's most listened-to stations. These will include three spots per hour between 8 A.M. and 7 P.M. for 3 days prior to the grand opening.
- **Business customers:** Direct mailings to all auto repair shops within the specified radius of the store will be made 1 week before opening. In addition to information about the opening, several promotional items will be given to those who show up (to be determined by store manager). Personal visits by team members will be made to all auto repair shops with more than 10 mechanics within that radius. Phone invitations will be made to all auto repair shops with between four and nine mechanics. Additional promotional incentives will be given to mechanics and managers of the larger businesses (to be determined by store manager).

John will need to bring these ideas to his client and principal stakeholder, Carol Byrnes, and begin the process of specifying exactly what the project will produce for the company. Working with Ms. Byrnes to clarify what the project will deliver is his all-important first step. As said earlier, John will also need to work with other stakeholders, like the store manager and a wide range of outside suppliers (e.g., the print media, mass mailers, and caterers), about what is doable and the associated costs. Of course, John will need to keep in close communication with his direct supervisor, Ralph, about his need for time to work on the project and to keep Ralph generally informed about project progress. Finally, John would do well to identify and contact others who have opened stores in the past. Although this opening is to be unlike any other, consulting with them to explore action areas, deliverables, and what is achievable, and to get any "words of wisdom," will likely yield a great deal of useful information. These plans, too, he will share with Carol Byrnes in her role as a key player in the host organization. Finally, in the hours before his meeting with Ms. Byrnes, John might make a few phone calls to see if he can get some early figures and information to bring to his meeting. A listing of key talking points for that meeting is given in Figure 2.1. Some of those points also touch on needed project resources and costs and the project's timeline—the topics we consider next.

Figure 2.1   Talking Points for the Meeting With Ms. Byrnes

- Mission statement
  - Project objectives and deliverables (action areas)
    - Where held (venue)
      Held at the store. What would Ms. Byrnes like to see included in the opening?
    - Advertising
      Several outlets possible (direct mail, radio, TV, newspaper, etc.)
      Any preferences?
    - Other
      What kinds of attendance have been considered "successful" in past openings?
      Are there any other action areas/project objectives or deliverables that need attention?

- Stakeholders
  - Ralph (talk with prior to meeting to discuss any issues)
  - Ms. Byrnes as client and host sponsor
    Explore the components of a successful opening
    Any strategic and tactical advice on conducting the project?
    Any other managers I need to touch base with?

- Project team
  How much of Tom's and Alice's time can be devoted to the project?
  What are their backgrounds? When can they start?
  Whom do I need to work with to OK their work with me?
- Store manager
  Will need to work closely with him or her. Plan to contact soon.
  What is standard practice in these kinds of working relationships?
  Any advice?
- Others?
  Who else do I need to work with?

• Budget
  - Cost figures: Will develop based on similar openings. Does Ms. Byrnes
    have a figure in mind (keep options open)?
  - Other issues?

• Timeline
  - Possible effects on deliverables (e.g., venue and advertising)
  - Other issues?

• Other resource issues
  - Previous project leaders (whom can I contact?)
  - Authority/support (from Ms. Byrnes within organization)
    Who needs to be notified of the project and me as its leader?
    Can I come to Ms. Byrnes if I need someone to "run interference"?

PROJECT PARAMETERS: PROJECT SCOPE, COSTS, AND TIMELINE

The project's mission statement and objectives address what the project is trying to achieve. The deliverables address the products and services that will be produced to achieve them. Three other basic elements now require attention: the project's scope and the resources it will take to produce those deliverables, what they will cost, and how long it will take.

PROJECT SCOPE

The **project scope** includes all those tasks necessary to produce the deliverables required. A final project plan will detail those tasks in the form of a work breakdown structure (addressed in the next chapter). At this stage, however, some basic estimates can be made about the work that will be required and, importantly, the resources needed to support that work. **Resources** include all products and services that the project team will need in order to produce project deliverables. Resources related to promotional requirements and the opening itself, for example, will affect the costs of John's project. Estimates of these certainly need to be made. Three other kinds of resources also require attention, however, in ways that are often overlooked. These include human resources, information, and authority.

Human resources—the project team—are needed, of course, to work on the project's activities. Beyond personnel costs, however, project leaders need to consider the knowledge, skills, and abilities needed to perform work on the project and just who possesses them. Good human resources are notoriously in short supply, and the earlier project leaders can "lock them in," the better.

John's Baltimore project presents another, quite common issue with human resources. Members of his project team—Tom and Alice—were "volunteered" by Ms. Byrnes. When working with the store manager, John may find yet another person has been "volunteered" for his team. As early as possible, project leaders need to check out the knowledge, skills, and abilities of such resources as well as their true availability and commitment to project work. When personnel are drawn from other parts of an organization, their time is usually committed to other projects. Both they and their supervisors are rarely happy to give *their* time to *your* project.

Information is another often overlooked resource that needs to be acquired as soon as possible. Because projects are unique endeavors, information that can be helpful in planning and conducting them is invaluable. One excellent source of information is experience—one's own and that of others. Even before detailed planning begins, it serves leaders well to consider others who have experience in working on and leading projects similar to the one being considered. This would include potential team members, of course, but also others who might be able to shed some light on the project. Even a few "cold calls" can reap tremendous gains in information. Those who have labored in the "project trenches" are often quite willing and even eager to share a few stories. In John's case, reaching out to one or two others who have been project leaders for opening other stores would be well worth the time. Networking from those project leaders to others they might recommend may be helpful as well.

Another important resource for any project is the authority required to make the decisions needed in a project. Projects, for example, often need the help of others. The authority to acquire their help can work wonders when needed. Authority comes from those higher up in the host organization who will actively champion project work. Their support needs to be acquired early in the planning process and maintained throughout the life of the project.

COSTS

Project costs are all the costs related to doing project work and acquiring its resource needs. For different reasons, project costs are always of concern to clients, the host organization, and project teams. Although ballpark figures tend to get discussed early on in projects, it is important to understand that early ballpark figures often determine stakeholders' expectations. Those expectations need to be handled carefully right from the beginning.[10]

Outside clients and even those in the host organization can underestimate true project costs. Outside clients, for example, tend to overlook a lot of project activities (e.g., the costs of simply administering a project) and underestimate the actual costs of project items (e.g., not considering Social Security, Medicare, and health benefits, among other personnel costs). Higher level managers in the host organization can also overlook cost items that are more apparent to project leaders working in the trenches (e.g., supplies, travel, overhead charges, equipment, and materials as well as administrative costs).

All this speaks to the fact that project leaders need to be very careful when dealing with project costs and the expectations of others. In John's case, he might get a reasonable ballpark figure by calling project leaders who have opened stores in the past, getting their final costs, and then adjusting for things like inflation and other items. This is called "top-down" or "analogous" budgeting, because it applies the costs of a similar project to the project at hand. The full costs, however, await "bottom-up" budgeting based on an accounting of all project tasks (these are addressed more fully in the next chapter).

Whether a project leader is asked to develop a project budget (as in John's case) or is given one by the performing organization, he or she needs to think through the implications in terms of deliverables and scheduled delivery very carefully and convey the implications to his or her manager and clients. This is a valuable service but one that often requires, at the same time, both tact and assertiveness.

TIMELINE

Like costs, the **project timeline**—the time allocated to get a project done—largely determines what *can* be done. Generally speaking, clients and host organizations want projects done as quickly as possible. Project teams, ever pressed for time, generally want more of it.

John's case is a typical one. Ms. Byrnes scheduled a hard completion date of June 15th without initial consultation with the project leader. That time horizon, however, might well affect some deliverables. A direct mail promotion, for example, might take more than 6 weeks to set up using standard operating procedures. Some equipment usually brought in for store openings may well be committed on that weekend by the vendors who supply it. Although more money can often speed things up or change the priorities of vendors, added costs, as we have seen, have issues of their own.

Project leaders need to make stakeholders aware of the implications of time demands just as they do for project costs. Like cost estimations, ballpark, top-down time horizons can be estimated from the times taken to complete similar projects. Nevertheless, each project is unique, and clients need to understand that time as well as costs will affect what deliverables are possible.

THE PROJECT CHARTER

Host organizations that routinely perform outside projects for their business often kick off a project with a project charter. A **project charter** is a thorough description of a project, and it formally authorizes the project to proceed. The idea of developing and using a project charter is a good one for all project leaders whether or not their organizations require one. A project charter can be as formal as those used in project organizations or as informal as a memo or e-mail that has been approved by the **project sponsor**—the manager with the authority to approve a project and commit organizational resources to it.

A project charter describes the project in enough detail that a sponsor can make an informed decision about whether it is worthwhile to commit resources to it. It describes the mission of a project and ties that mission to the broader organizational purpose(s) of the mission—why the project is worthwhile to the host organization. The project charter also lays out what will be needed for the project by first tying the project mission to the project's main objectives and deliverables. It then goes on to lay out expected timelines and enough cost information that all stakeholders can make an informed decision to move ahead. A project charter should also address what will be needed to make the project successful. Time and budget needs are based on time and cost estimates. Human and other resources needed are described. What levels of authority are needed to conduct project activities should be considered, as well as any other assumptions critical to project success (e.g., the availability of key personnel).

Just the production of such a charter will force the project leader to consider the important elements of the project at its initiation. The formal acceptance of the charter by key stakeholders, however, signals to the project leader that the project can, indeed, move ahead as planned. It signals, as well, that the project is a legitimate undertaking that has the full backing it needs to achieve its goals. Table 2.2 presents some key questions leaders can use as a check-off list when first developing a project. Although the questions are not exhaustive, they provide a jumping-off point for project leaders as they begin to put projects together for the first time.

Table 2.2   Initiation Check-Off List

There are many issues to consider when first planning a project. Listed here are a few of the more important questions leaders should ask themselves as they move through the project initiation process. The questions are meant to encourage project leaders to think through the issues involved and are meant to be used as a point of departure rather than as a comprehensive listing.

- What is the mission or purpose of the project?
- What are the key project objectives?
- What are the client's final and interim deliverables? Show extra care in the development of these; they are your "contracted" items. For example, are there any special quality requirements?
- What is the basic scope of project work that will need to be done? Consider work to produce the deliverables and any administrative requirements.
- What resources will be required? Consider human resources, material, equipment, facilities, and any other resource that may be needed. Include consideration of subcontracts for outsourcing. Consider any special arrangements that may be needed.
- What is the timeline for the project? Can the project be completed in that time?
- What is the budget for the project? Will it cover the costs required?
- What are the key areas of risk for the project in terms of deliverables, work requirements, costs, and time?
- Who are the key stakeholders of this project? What are their requirements? To what extent can they affect the project? Consider the client, higher management (including your direct supervisor), others on the project team, end users, external vendors, and internal suppliers of project resources. Make sure you have contacted all relevant stakeholders, whether or not they are key players. Make sure you have extended discussions with key players about their expectations.
- Whom can you quickly contact to get information about projects similar to this one? Ask about deliverables, project scope of work, timelines, budget, and special or unforeseen problems that arose that you should consider in your own risk assessments. Ask for referrals to others who have had similar projects whom you can contact.

(Continued)

Table 2.2 (Continued)

- Have you developed a written charter of the project? Has it been approved by the key stakeholders of the project? Has it been formally accepted and approved by those in management who have the authority to approve the project and allocate funds and other organizational resources for its budget?

Once the charter is developed and accepted, it can be used as the basis for developing a full project plan. The project plan will nail down project specifics and guide the project through its life cycle. We will be attending to the other elements of the project plan in the following chapters, but it is appropriate now to specify just what goes into a project plan.

THE PROJECT PLAN

Before they begin actual construction, contractors need blueprints of the building they are to construct. So, too, do project leaders need their own blueprints of the project—the **project plan**. Project plans will vary in content, complexity, and detail depending on the projects they address. At the very least, however, a project plan should include a number of common elements.

- **The project's mission statement:** The mission statement lays out the general purpose of the project. The general purpose of the project needs to be tied to the broader objectives and mission of the host organization.

- **The project's objectives:** What the project is trying to achieve in specific terms. These are made relevant to the project's mission statement.

- **All deliverables and quality criteria:** Deliverables include both the final set of deliverables to be given to the client and all interim deliverables. If required, any quality criteria or other specifications for those deliverables should be included.

- **A complete work breakdown structure:** This is a complete specification of all project work that needs to be done—the project's scope. We cover this in Chapter 3.

- **The project schedule:** This is a schedule showing which tasks are to be done by what dates in the project. Typically, the schedule specifies the start and end or completion dates for all project tasks. We cover this in Chapter 4.

- **All resources needed for the project:** These include human resources, materials, equipment, facilities, and the like.[11]

- **The project's budget:** The budget should be laid out by project task so it can be used to control costs throughout the project as those tasks are performed.

- **Risk assessments:** Project risks include those that threaten the attainment of project objectives, push back project dates, increase project costs, or detrimentally affect project deliverables. These are addressed in a project risk plan, which we cover in Chapter 5.

The project plan, then, is really a series of project documents. Whether they are kept in three-ring binders or on a computer, project leaders will continuously refer to them as the project moves forward. They will also keep updating the plan as changes are required. They will add other documents to the plan as well—authorization for changes, sign-offs for work done, and the like. Keeping track of all these documents is an important administrative task for project leaders. They always seem to come in handy down the road and are often required by one or more key stakeholders.

As we finish this chapter, we see that our project charter has given us a good start at creating our project plan. Its purpose, after all, was to give stakeholders a ballpark idea of the project in enough detail to allow a decision to move forward and make a commitment to the project the leader had envisioned. We turn now to developing the work breakdown structure of the project plan and how it is used to make the more precise estimates leaders need of the resource, cost, and time demands of the project.

SUMMARY

All projects have a mission. That mission is to help address the problems and needs of the project's clients. Mission statements clarify the goals and aims of a project in those terms. As such, they help give general guidance to a project. They help to orient and direct project teams, for example, and anyone else who might work with or contribute to a project. When they are developed in concert with a project's principal stakeholders, mission statements provide a common understanding of the project that can help tie together the often diverse interests of stakeholders. This common ground can be used in bringing together stakeholders to negotiate matters of common concern as needed.

All projects also have a number of stakeholders who have a vested interest in the mission of a project. The client, of course, has a stake in the project solving his or her problem. The organization hosting the project has a stake in seeing the project run smoothly and, if appropriate, making a profit. The project team is a stakeholder, including the project leader. The team members want to see the project become a success, of course, but they would like not to be overstretched and overcommitted in doing so. End users are those who will ultimately use the output of the project. Suppliers are stakeholders, too. External suppliers make money from supplying a project. Internal suppliers, on the other hand, often have to supply resources to projects without compensation, putting a strain on the project-supplier relationship that needs attention. In all cases, stakeholders are people—people who can make decisions that can have an important effect on the project. Project leaders, then, need to be able to work with them successfully.

Once a project's mission has been clarified by its stakeholders, project objectives and deliverables need to be specified. Project objectives are specific goals that must be attained for the mission to be achieved. Deliverables are the products and services that will fulfill those specific goals. Project objectives and deliverables are better when they are SMART: specific, measurable, actionable, realistic, and time-specific.

Project objectives and deliverables help the client see the project in concrete terms, and they provide the project team with clear direction. They also help often diverse stakeholders negotiate concrete project outcomes that will satisfy their interests. Project leaders need to help their stakeholders come to agreement about what specific objectives and deliverables will satisfy them before moving ahead.

Once a project's mission, objectives, and deliverables have clarified its direction, project leaders need to make initial assessments of a project's work requirements or its project scope, its resource needs, its costs, and its timeline. All projects require resources to get them done, and an initial estimate needs to be made of them. Key among these are human resources—people with the knowledge, skills, and abilities to get the project done. In addition to all the other resources a project needs, two other, often overlooked, resources are information useful for the project and the authority to take the actions needed when conducting the project. A little time invested in attention to these resources can reap large benefits later.

All project stakeholders are interested in project costs—each for his or her own reasons and concerns. Initial ballpark estimates for projects will be needed, but care must be taken that the expectations of stakeholders are not inflated. Project leaders can often get an initial ballpark estimate by top-down or analogous estimating. To do so, a similar project is selected, its final costs are noted, and then they are modified to fit the specifics of the present project.

Stakeholders are also interested in the amount of time it will take to complete a project. As with cost estimates, a top-down time estimate can be developed from similar projects adjusted for present circumstances. Often both costs and a project's timeline are simply given to a project leader. In these cases, it is best for the leader to clarify the implications of such explicit and firm constraints on project deliverables.

Before a proposed project gets fully under way, the leader should develop a project charter. The project charter describes what the project is trying to achieve and how it intends to do so. It includes estimated costs and a project schedule or timeline as well as a description of needed resources. Once a sponsoring manager in the host organization or the leader's client formally sanctions the charter, the project has the agreement of key stakeholders to move forward the full planning and execution of the project.

The project charter is the first step in producing a project plan—the blueprint project leaders use to fully understand and run a project. At the very least, a project plan consists of a mission statement and the project's objectives. It should also contain a complete breakdown of all project work, along with a schedule of when specific tasks will be done. Resource needs require attention as well as a project budget. Finally, assessments need to be made regarding various risks to the project—threats to deliverables, costs, and time required for the project.

REVIEW QUESTIONS

1. Define and characterize mission statements. What roles do mission statements play for a project?

2. Describe how mission statements help to establish common ground.

3. What is a stakeholder in a project? Who are the stakeholders reviewed in this chapter, and what are their concerns or interests in a project?

4. What are the objectives and deliverables in a project? How do they differ from one another and from the mission statement? What roles do objectives and deliverables play for a project?

5. What are some of the key resources that need to be considered early in the development of a project?

6. How might ballpark estimates of project costs be developed early in the project? How should cost estimates be handled when working with the project's stakeholders?

7. What is a project charter? What forms can a project charter take? What are reasons that a project charter should be developed and used?

EXERCISE

1. Work individually or as a team to develop a project charter.

   a. Focus on a project that is relevant to you or your team.

   b. Focus on and define the basic problems the project will address.

   c. Identify the major stakeholders in the project and their interests.

   d. Develop a mission statement for the project and its major objectives. Develop one or more project deliverables for each project objective.

   e. Identify some of the key resources you will need for the project. Be as specific and concrete as possible given the needs of your project.

   f. Estimate the costs and time needed for the project. These estimates are for purposes of writing up the project charter only.

   g. Write up a one- to two-page charter for the project. Frame the charter as a proposal for approval by higher management in your host organization or by your client.

ENDNOTES

1. The Project Management Institute uses *customer* to indicate the client. Throughout this book, the term *client* is used.

2. The term *performing organization* is the one used by: Project Management Institute. (2008). *A guide to the project management body of knowledge* (4th ed.). Newtown Square, PA: Author. *Host organization* is the label preferred here, but *performing organization* is also used.

3. These kinds of projects, in fact, account for a great deal of the growth in the demand for project leaders.

4. A careful reader might note that the June 15th date set by Carol Byrnes has been changed to "on or about." Project leaders often take such constraints as "given" without question. Although Ms. Byrnes no doubt has this date in mind, further preliminary work may find it unacceptable. For example, some other event might be occurring on that date that would undermine the whole purpose of the opening (e.g., an automotive show attracting business users of the store or a NASCAR event attracting retail customers of the store).

5. In the development of a new product, for example, interim deliverables may include prototypes, testing, and marketing plans as well as the end product itself. Quite often, interim deliverables are required to decide whether to proceed with the project. We will see in the next chapter, as well, that the project can produce deliverables for itself in the form of planning and administrative products and services. Projects may also purchase some of their deliverables.

6. A common mistake, in fact, is for managers to simply dictate objectives to project leaders early on without carefully thinking them through. If so, project

leaders need to review the given objectives to see their full implications. These need to be brought to the attention of the manager privately and, hopefully, before the manager makes any public declarations of the project's objectives.

7. While the acronym "SMART" is a common one, the "A" has been used to refer to a number of goal criteria. *Achievable, accurate, agreed-upon,* and *action-oriented* are a few of them. I prefer *actionable* as it is least redundant and focuses attention on making things happen.

8. Using a "single text" procedure is one way of approaching this issue. The project leader lays out an initial listing of objectives and deliverables and lets the stakeholders discuss among themselves how to alter it. As they do so, the project leader facilitates negotiations with what can and cannot be done and addresses the interests of each stakeholder in terms of the project's mission. The stakeholders themselves, then, assume the responsibility for negotiating their own agreement.

9. These are two very different kinds of project objectives. The promotional objective is a performance objective—a measure of how well the advertising deliverable is to perform. The second objective—customers attending—is a measure of overall project success or the extent to which the deliverables produce what the client ultimately wants. Importantly, performance objectives of project deliverables are more under the control of a project than whether those deliverables will achieve other "downstream" aims. Any number of factors, completely out of control of the project team, can affect those kinds of objectives. For this reason, project leaders often try to limit project objectives to performance objectives or simply specifications of deliverables without regard to how well they are to perform. Clients, however, will judge a project in terms of how well deliverables meet their ultimate needs.

10. It should be mentioned that the costs of a project are very different from the price of a project. The costs of a project are borne by the host or performing organization. The price of a project is what the host organization charges the client and includes other associated overhead costs and profits to be made. Project leaders in host organizations rarely discuss costs with outside clients and are usually not involved in the pricing of a project at all.

11. Unique resources are particularly important to include. If you need a particular person to work on some task because of his or her singular expertise, that should be noted and arranged far in advance. The same goes for any special equipment, materials, and so forth.

KEY TERMS

Client: the customer—person or organization—for which the project is being conducted and the ultimate source of funds and resources for the project.

Deliverables: specific products and services produced to achieve project objectives.

End Users: the people who will ultimately use or benefit from a project.

Host Organization: the organization in which the project is conducted.

Key Stakeholders: stakeholders who have the power and authority to make important decisions about the conduct and outcomes of the project.

Mission Statement: a few sentences or paragraphs that state the general purpose and aims of a project—what it is trying to achieve.

Project Charter: a thorough description of a project used to formally authorize the project to proceed.

Project Costs: all the costs related to doing project work and acquiring its resource needs.

Project Objectives: specific goals or outcomes a project needs to achieve to fulfill its mission.

Project Plan: the "blueprint" that project leaders use to fully understand and run a project. It includes the project's mission, objectives, and deliverables. A work breakdown structure of work requirements is also included with the project schedule and budget to cover all project costs. All required resources are specified and assessments of foreseeable project risk provided.

Project Scope: all the tasks necessary to produce the deliverables required.

Project Sponsor: the manager within the host organization who has the authority to approve a project and commit organizational resources to it.

Project Team: the group of people who actually carry out project activities.

Project Timeline: the time required to complete a project.

Resources: products and services that the project team will need in order to produce project's deliverables.

SMART: project objectives and deliverables should be specific, measurable, actionable, realistic, time-specific.

Stakeholders: those people, organizational units, and institutions that have a vested interest in the project and can affect it in some way.

Suppliers: people who deliver the products and services that the team itself cannot supply.

3

The Work Breakdown Structure

INTRODUCTION

THE COMPLIANCE PROJECT

Linda Swain had been recently hired by AgenCorp as director for its elder care center in Portland, Oregon: Golden Years. AgenCorp had been acquiring elder care facilities across the country, and the Portland facility was one of its larger acquisitions with well over a hundred beds. Linda was a registered nurse with a great deal of experience from "floor care" to higher levels of nursing administration in larger facilities like this one. She replaced the last director, who was let go by AgenCorp. In addition to the usual duties of a director, Linda was charged to remedy a number of problems held over from the previous owners. One of these problems was potentially "fatal" for Golden Years: threatened decertification by the state of Oregon. In the two previous inspections, Golden Years had received a score of "no pass" based on a number of violations ranging across all operations of the center. One of Linda's most pressing projects on being hired was to make sure Golden Years passed the state inspection on its next 6-month review.

The mission of Linda's Compliance Project was pretty clear. Golden Years must pass the next state inspection in 6 months. After looking into the matter, Linda was able to put together more specific project objectives as well. State certification addressed each of the five main divisions of AgenCorp's facility: administration, food service/nutrition, physical therapy, medical care, and hospitality services. Passing certifications in these five areas presented themselves as natural project objectives. The state inspection criteria for each area provided Linda with the detail she would need to make the project objectives and deliverables specific and measurable. In addition, Linda decided that she wanted to establish standard operating procedures (SOPs) for each division to make sure Golden Years would pass state inspections in the future.

The challenge now was to figure out what specific tasks needed to be done to achieve those objectives. Along with identifying the necessary tasks to be completed, Linda would need to know who would do them, what resources they would need to get the job done, what everything would cost, and how to organize the project so she could exercise proper command and control of it. All these rest on developing a work breakdown structure of the project—the focus of this chapter.

CHAPTER OVERVIEW

Projects are unique, one-of-a-kind endeavors. Even when a project leader has determined what to deliver, figuring out how to do it can be overwhelming. The principal approach to use in addressing any large problem is to break it down into smaller ones. The same goes for projects. Linda's first step was to break the project mission—Golden Years needs to pass certification–into its major objectives: Golden Years needs to pass certification in each of its five divisions and develop SOPs for each area to pass in the future. The task now was to break down those objectives into the larger jobs needed to achieve them and then to lay out the more detailed tasks to get each larger job done. The result of this process is called a work breakdown structure, and it forms the foundation of any project. In this chapter, we take a close look at what work breakdown structures are and the roles they play in projects. We then go on to discuss how to construct them and wrap up by addressing some of the ways work breakdown structures are used.

THE WORK BREAKDOWN STRUCTURE AND ITS PROJECT ROLE

According to the Project Management Institute, a **work breakdown structure** (WBS) is "a deliverable-oriented hierarchical decomposition of the work to be executed by the project team to accomplish the project objectives and create the required deliverables. It organizes and defines the total scope of the project."[1] Another way of putting this is that a WBS itemizes all those tasks that must be done to complete the project—to produce its deliverables. Those tasks are laid out in a hierarchy of larger jobs to get done, the smaller tasks needed to do those larger jobs, and so on in more and more detail until one gets to the most detailed tasks needed.

Figure 3.1 shows part of what Linda's WBS might look like. The mission of the Compliance Project is to pass state certification in 6 months and to produce SOPs to do so in the future. This mission is broken down into five basic project objectives. Each organizational division—Administration, Physical Therapy, Food and Nutrition, Medical Care, and Hospitality Services—is to pass certification and develop its own SOPs (breakdowns for Physical

Figure 3.1   Illustration of a Work Breakdown Structure for Golden Years Compliance Project

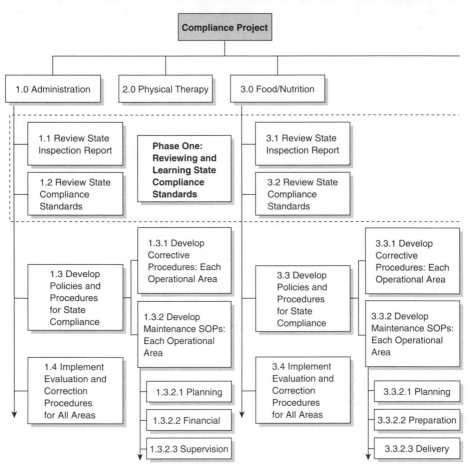

(Continued)

Therapy and Hospitality Services are not shown for reasons of space). You might also note there are breakdowns for Project Planning and Project Administration. These address project support activities, which we will cover later.

To pass certification and develop SOPs for the future, Linda has determined that each area will need to review its earlier inspections to target past and possible future problems ("Review State Inspection Report": 1.1, 2.1, 3.1, 4.1, and 5.1). A deliverable for each of these tasks might be a brief report detailing those problems. Another task that Linda believes each area should

Figure 3.1 (Continued)

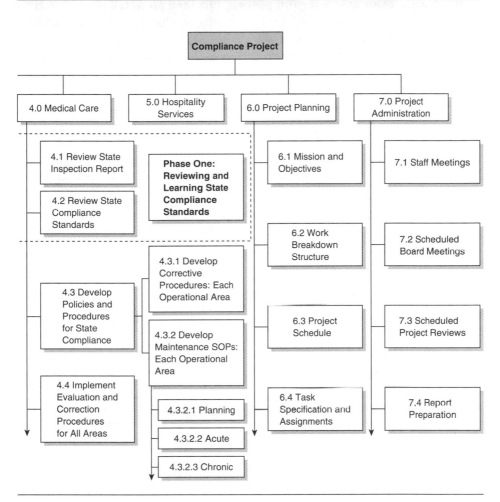

NOTE: SOP = standard operating procedure.

do is to "Review State Compliance Standards" for its area (1.2, 2.2, 3.2, 4.2, and 5.2). This task might produce a number of deliverables including a briefing report to be given at a meeting of division heads and an initial check-off list to be used later in developing the area's SOPs. Finally, Linda believes both reviews need to be completed before anything else can be done toward certification. Together, then, the tasks will compose Phase One of the Compliance Project. This kind of graphical representation of a WBS can serve a variety of purposes. We will come back to it throughout Chapter 3.

ROLES PLAYED BY A WBS

It is hard to overstate the importance of a WBS for a project. It is the foundation of virtually everything relevant to actually conducting it. Laying out the scope of project tasks that need to be done; estimating what it will take to do those tasks; and helping to show how tasks, people, and other project elements are to be organized into a project structure are some of the more important roles played by a WBS discussed here.

Lays Out the Scope of Project Work

As noted in Chapter 2, the scope of work in a project is the sum total of all work that must be done to accomplish its goals. It does not take long to realize that a project's true scope is probably not completely understood until it is fully broken down into its component tasks. An important goal of a WBS, then, is to make sure that all the tasks necessary to complete a project are identified before the project actually begins.

Provides the Foundation of All Project Estimates

Only after a project has been broken down to the detail of project tasks can a project leader get a precise, bottom-up estimate of what it will take to complete the project. These include any resource requirements, the time it is likely to take to do the project, the costs of each task, and assessments of risk—the chances of actually producing the deliverables on time and on budget. Although a project leader might have a good guess about what it may take to complete a particular project component, he or she will not have a precise estimate until it is based on a WBS.

Helps to Provide the Organizational Structure of the Project

Once a project is broken down into its tasks, it can be "put back together" again into a project structure. The Compliance Project shown in Figure 3.1 probably reminds you of an organizational chart.[2] That is no coincidence. Managers and project leaders both go through the same kind of "ends-to-means" analysis to put their organizations and projects together. What they are trying to accomplish—their goals—are the ends they want to achieve. Next, they need to find the means to achieve them. In the case of a project, the project's mission is its ultimate goal, and project goals are designed to achieve it. Project deliverables—the products and services the project will actually produce—are the means to achieve those objectives. Next, the project deliverables themselves play the role of ends; and they, in turn, need to be broken down into the basic jobs—the means—to develop or produce them. Those jobs are generally large and made up of many smaller tasks. They will need to be broken down, then, into smaller and smaller jobs until it is pretty clear what exactly needs to be done. The end result is the work breakdown structure—a collection of project tasks and "work packages" that define the most detailed work of the project.

Going back to the Compliance Project in Figure 3.1, the ultimate goal is passing state certification and developing SOPs to do so in the future. Each division passing certification and developing its own SOPs are the means to achieve that end. Each area passing its own certification now becomes an end in itself, and other tasks become the means to achieve it. And so it goes until the WBS is complete and the tasks are ready to be arranged into a project structure.

In summary, a WBS is a comprehensive listing of all project work. Once a project is broken down into its component tasks, leaders are better able to assess the true scope of work needed to get it done. They are also better able to assess its resource, time, and cost requirements. Another important outcome of a WBS is a project structure that will facilitate the kinds of resource allocation, staffing and delegation, and related command and control needs of a project. The **project structure** is created by reassembling the tasks broken down in a WBS in a way that helps the allocation of project work and the command and control of the project.

PRODUCING A WBS

The technical name for breaking down jobs into ever smaller tasks is "**decomposition**." Larger jobs are decomposed into all the tasks needed to complete the job. This is usually done step by step with progressively more and more detail. The point at which leaders stop is when they believe they have enough task detail to reasonably estimate things like personnel and other resource needs, the true costs of the task, and the risks associated with getting that particular task done.[3,4]

Although this can be a very straightforward process, errors often occur. Chief among them is to forget some task or set of tasks that needs to be done to complete the project or some of its components. Being people, after all, project leaders can overlook things, and they have their blind spots too. It is a good idea, then, for project leaders to bring in other experts to review the tasks that need to be done. If these experts can include key members of the project, leaders get a double benefit: expert advice and an early start at organizing and orienting the important members of the project team itself.

When developing a WBS, project leaders have a natural tendency to focus on the core tasks of the project. Often overlooked, however, are the necessary support tasks to pull off a project on time and on budget.

Core Tasks

Core tasks are all those tasks necessary to produce the products and services that will be delivered to the client. These tend to command the most project attention because clients and the host organization are most concerned about them. Despite the attention they command, many core tasks are overlooked when producing a WBS. People tend to think of those tasks most directly related to producing a good or a service, for example, but tend to overlook logistical or preparatory work for those tasks. In Linda's case, the top staff will need copies of the state's compliance policies and, likely, more user-friendly reviews of them. Linda may even need to provide training for herself and her top staff to fully understand state policies, criteria, and inspection procedures. Securing those reviews and providing that training can be easily overlooked as important considerations in breaking the project's work down.

When breaking down core activities, then, it pays to move through the tasks in a deliberate way, thinking of all the related activities needed to achieve the higher level goal. Reaching out to others can be a real benefit to leaders in this endeavor. Those who have conducted similar projects or project components can provide valuable information. Those who will actually do the project work can be of help too. Their operational experience can help flesh out the work needed to complete their individual objectives and deliverables. Because they will actually be charged with doing the work, they are usually motivated to be thorough.

Support Tasks

Support tasks are all those tasks necessary for conducting the project itself. They are the most overlooked components of project work, and they need to be included in every WBS for at least two reasons. First, like any task, they consume time and resources. Somebody *will* pay for them; the only question is who. The client is unlikely to pay for unplanned expenses, and your host organization will be far from happy to do so. That leaves the project leader and project team to pay—most often with uncompensated overtime! Second, support work needs to be done so the project runs smoothly. Without proper support, work on the core components of a project will suffer. Two basic kinds of support activities are project planning and project administration.

Project Planning

Project planning is really the first phase of any project, and it involves all those tasks that we are addressing in the first section of this book and more. Quite often, project planning is viewed as a kind of overhead. Basic planning needs to be done before a project is approved (e.g., to produce the project charter), and developing a more detailed project plan is needed before actually running or executing the project. Clients are often reluctant to pay for a project plan that may not suit their needs. Project planning takes time, however, and it consumes resources and costs money. When project leaders are asked to lay out plans for a project, they need to be aware that they will be consuming a fair amount of resources to do so. They need strategies, then, not to carry the effort too far without reimbursement or increased possibilities that the project will, in fact, go forward.

One basic strategy is to plan incrementally. Once a mission statement has been developed, project objectives laid out, and a best-guess estimate made of costs and time for the project, it is time to pause and reflect whether the project is worth moving forward as it was initially conceived. Host organizations that routinely conduct project work generally have SOPs to do just this sort of thing. Projects go through an initiating process of initial planning that results in a project charter, as discussed in Chapter 2. Key stakeholders use the initial plan of the charter to decide whether to approve further work on the project, and then keep track as the planning moves forward. The whole idea is to decide whether a project is worth the effort early in the project cycle rather than later on when too many resources have already been expended.

This process can be followed in other, less formal project situations as well. When handed a project by one's boss, for example, quick preliminary estimates of work scope, costs, time estimates, and likely benefits should be shared with him or her as soon as possible. As another example, if a consultant is working with a client on a new project, the consultant might include an initial charge for project planning to some agreed level of detail. Once those plans are developed, the project reaches a decision point at which both the client and the consultant as project leader decide whether to move forward. If so, the initial planning charge can be rolled into the overall project cost structure. The important point here is to keep the key stakeholders informed about the project costs from the very beginning, get them on board, and "track" them through the planning process until they literally—as well as psychologically—buy into it.

Project Administration

Another support process often overlooked is **project administration**. Even small projects can generate a number of administrative tasks, and those tasks seem to increase exponentially as project size increases. Quite a few administrative tasks are associated with complying with the rules and regulations of the host organization. Leaders, for example, are often required to keep track of and report on their project's costs and budget expenditures. Other administrative tasks are required for project communications. Project meetings with staff, clients, and others, for example, can take a great deal of project work and consume a great deal of personnel time. Command and control activities also require time and resource expenditures. Most projects have milestones included in their schedules to indicate when certain tasks are to be done. Although milestones are defined as "no resource use" events, preparing for them usually consumes quite a bit of resources in conducting compliance checks and corrections, developing reports, and meeting with clients or project leaders. Formally including support activities in the project's WBS, then, is necessary.

In summary, producing the project's WBS defines the scope of project work in real, concrete terms. Quite often, however, tasks are overlooked, even critical ones. Part of the reason is time. Project leaders are pressured to begin project work before the project itself is fully laid out. Another reason is technical. Because a project is a unique, one-of-a-kind endeavor, all the necessary tasks to get it done have not yet been developed. Still a third reason is human. Project leaders have their own blind spots and can become impatient. We tend to overlook things we take for granted when we want to move on with our projects. Project leaders need to remember, however, that they and their project teams are likely to bear most of the cost of overlooked work. That fact alone should encourage leaders to reflect a little longer and reach out to others to make sure the WBS is complete. Those others include experts in the technical areas of project work, those who have had experience in similar project work, and those who will be actually working on the project producing the deliverables envisioned.

The Compliance Project is a case in point. Linda Swain might well consider bringing in an outside consultant with expertise in certification during the initial planning stages as well as later in the project. She might also consider taking her counterpart at another elder care center out to lunch to chat about the project, particularly if her counterpart has had similar experiences with certification. Finally, Linda would do well to discuss her plans with her seconds-in-command to better assess the tasks that likely lie ahead as well as bring them on board early in the planning process. A few hours invested in these kinds of consultation activities early in the project will likely save Linda endless problems further down the road.

USING THE WBS

One of the very nice things about constructing a WBS is that it focuses a project leader's attention in useful ways. First, attention is focused on the broader project and its major objectives and deliverables. Next, attention is focused on the major jobs that must be done to produce each deliverable. This process continues until attention is finally focused on the actual work tasks or work packages themselves.

Once the work packages are broken out, the project leader can better estimate what it will take to get the project done. The leader can also begin the task of reassembling those tasks into a coherent project structure that he or she can use as part of the project plan. The project plan, in turn, plays a critical role in effectively directing and controlling the project itself. We will look first at the kinds of estimates project leaders make using their WBS to guide them. We conclude by examining how the tasks in a WBS can be used to create a project structure suitable for work allocation and command and control.

RESOURCE, TIME, AND COST ESTIMATES

There are two basic ways of developing estimates in projects: top-down or analogous estimating and bottom-up estimating. **Top-down** or **analogous estimating** looks at actual resource, time, and cost estimates of similar projects or project components. These estimates are used as a base, and adjustments are made to reflect the conditions of the present project. There are two primary benefits to this approach. One is that estimates can be made fairly quickly if records have been kept of previous project work. Another advantage is that this technique benefits from hindsight. Project leaders can overlook any number of things when estimating the resources, time, or costs of a project before it is actually done. Because analogous estimating makes use of information from tasks that are already completed, however, everything that may have been overlooked has made itself known. The principal drawback of this method is that previous projects reflect previous conditions and needs. The present project, even if similar, is nevertheless unique. It can differ in substantial ways that may be overlooked unless more detailed estimating is used. This problem is made worse when estimates rely more on memory than on records and when the differences of the current project are not properly considered.

Bottom-up estimating looks at each task itself and estimates the resources, time, and cost to do it from a "zero base." For each task in the WBS, for example, the costs of human resources, equipment, material, and other charges are calculated and rolled up for the entire project. The principal advantage of this approach is precision. When all tasks and task elements have been identified, more precise estimates can be made. Still another advantage is that bottom-up estimating focuses the leader's attention on the costs of each work package. This kind of detailed information is necessary for developing a project budget to keep track of costs as the project moves ahead. A principal drawback is that this approach takes a fair amount of time and resources itself. Another drawback is that, quite often, task elements and even entire tasks are overlooked in developing a WBS, which affects the precision that bottom-up estimating promises.

It is likely best to combine the two approaches when estimating resource, time, and cost elements of any project. Bottom-up estimating brings potential precision, and analogous estimating brings past experience to the whole process. In any event, estimating project needs is itself a project activity that consumes resources, takes time, and costs money. At some point, a trade-off must be made between ever-elusive precision and good-enough estimates to move forward. When estimating resource, time, and cost requirements, however, project leaders should keep a few things in mind.

Estimating Resources

Resource estimates generally focus on the human resources, equipment, and materials needed to do the job. Human resource assessments tend to focus on the project team members because they usually are the ones doing most of the work. The knowledge, skills, and abilities needed to produce the task's deliverables should be considered, as well as the number of personnel needed to finish on time. These estimates are then used for later personnel decisions, cost estimates, and scheduling.

Outside personnel needed to complete a job should also be considered. Those who charge the project for their contributions tend to get the most attention, for obvious reasons. Linda, for example, plans to have trainers and consultants help in the Compliance Project. Often, however, host organizations volunteer their own people to help with the project in some way or another. Even if the organization does not charge the project for these personnel, you can bet the people involved and their supervisors care. They care because they must take time off from their own work to do the project's work. The number of hours needed from them, then, requires careful thought, with due consideration given to their other duties. Other kinds of outside human resources also need to be considered. Outside regulators, for example, are often needed to certify the quality of work or the quality of the work environment. Projects may or may not bear the actual costs of such reviews. Even if they do not, it is best to include them in the WBS as a no-cost activity to keep track of them for later scheduling.

The contributions of one more project member, in particular, are often overlooked—contributions required from the project leader. The project leader needs to assess the extent to which he or she will be needed in any particular task. We will address delegation in another chapter, and project leaders should not have to closely supervise every task. Nevertheless, project leaders have a number of tasks that they lead (e.g., planning, conducting project meetings, and performing budget reviews, to name a few). Project leaders also have quality control, command and control, and other responsibilities that require their attention (e.g., reporting project milestones, communicating and negotiating with stakeholders, hiring and training personnel, and meeting with clients). Project leaders need to consider their own time, then, as a limited resource that needs careful allocation.

After estimating the necessary human resources, the project team must estimate equipment and material resource needs as well. Any special equipment or materials needed to do the task must be carefully considered. The importance of getting the right tools and materials to the right workers at the right time is often underappreciated. The logistics behind this task can be quite complex and sometimes seen as boring and ignored. They often play an important, even critical role, however, in finishing a project on time and on budget.

Finally, other needed resources are sometimes simply assumed to be available. Office space, office equipment, and supplies, for example, are often overlooked in planning. In many cases, they are made available by the host organization. If the project is occurring offsite, however, resources like these cannot be assumed. Not to be forgotten are intangible resources like information and authority. Information is always a prized resource in projects because each project is unique. Linda, for example, is willing to pay a great deal of money for information about certification (i.e., the trainers) and information about the extent to which her project will actually meet state standards (i.e., with an initial, "shakedown" review by an outside consultant). As a project leader walks through the tasks of a project, information needs should be considered as well. So, too, should the requisite authority to do a project task. Often, project tasks must be done in organizational arenas outside of the scope of a lead person's authority. Although Linda does not need to worry too much about the scope of her authority for this project, those who report to her may have to. The project duties they perform may well take them beyond their normal areas of authority, and they will need higher level authority to complete those duties.

Estimating Time Requirements

Overall project timelines are often given at the project level. Linda has 6 months, for example, to meet state certification standards. Clients usually have an idea about when they would like to see a project completed. Estimating the time requirements for individual project tasks is the first step in arranging those tasks to complete the project on time.

Given a certain level of human and other resources, project leaders can estimate how long project tasks will take. Information from similar tasks, set standards, input from the team itself, and the leader's own experience are all inputs to this estimate. In addition to this best guess, the leader may wish to provide pessimistic and optimistic estimates of completion times. This creates a range of time within which the leader is reasonably sure the task will be completed. Pessimistic and optimistic estimates are, in fact, used in the Project Evaluation and Review Technique (PERT) for scheduling to help adjust for the "time risk" of projects (see Chapter 4). Even if the leader does not use PERT, it is a good idea to estimate a time range for task completion.

This is a good time, too, to consider lag times for a task. **Lag time** is the amount of time a task needs to "rest" after work has been done on it. For example, once concrete has been poured, smoothed, and finished, it must be left for some time to cure. The job is not really done until the curing time has passed. When thinking through the tasks of a project, then, this kind of required downtime needs to be considered. Some tasks may require advance time as well. For example, a vendor may require advance notification that material is needed before it can be delivered, or an inspector may require a 30-day notice to schedule her inspection visit.

Estimating Costs

For each detailed task in the WBS, the costs of human resources, equipment, materials, and other charges are calculated and combined for the project as a whole. Care must be taken, however, to include all cost items. Often overlooked costs include travel, long-distance communications, fees charged by regulatory agencies or vendors, inflation adjustments (for multiyear projects), organizational overhead charges, and the like. Table 3.1 gives an example of a spreadsheet layout detailing some costs for one element of the Compliance Project—consultant reviews of Linda's operations and a feedback report. Similar spreadsheets can be used by project leaders to detail their costs once the project's work has been broken down.

All cost estimates have risk associated with them. One of the most important risks facing the project team is the danger of underestimating the actual

Table 3.1   Project Costs: Illustration of One Task Cost Estimate

7.6: Consultant Review of Operations and Feedback Report

Resource	Quantity	Usage	Cost per Unit	Total Item Cost
Personnel				
Director	1	1 day	$250.00/day	$250.00
Head nurse	4	1 day	150.00/day	600.00
Support nurse	8	2 days	100.00/day	1,600.00
Support staff	4	1 day	60.00	240.00
Equipment				
Computers	8	2 days	00.00	00.00
Materials				
Standard operating procedure manuals each area	5	25 manuals	00.00	00.00
Other (specify)				
Consultants	2	2 days	1,000.00	4,000.00
Travel	2	1 round trip each	1,000.00	2,000.00
Lodging	2	2 days	125.00	500.00
Report	1		500.00	500.00
Overhead charges	Included			
Total resource costs				$9,690.00

costs of the project. In that case, the project team or host organization will have to bear the costs of project completion. It is quite common, then, to add a risk adjustment to the calculated costs for each task that helps to offset that risk. Overestimating project costs also presents a risk: the client going somewhere else to do business. Clients often press project leaders to keep costs down while pressing for product quality in the shortest possible time. A careful cost analysis can help leaders clarify project costs to their clients so that they can appreciate what it takes to produce quality work.

DEVELOPING A PROJECT STRUCTURE

Once project tasks are broken out into a WBS, they can be reassembled into a project structure. One important use of this structure is that it lets everyone know how they and their work fit into the project and how others depend on them. Another important use is for **command and control** of the project—the use of project authority to monitor and control the use of resources to achieve project objectives.

Figure 3.1 shows the Compliance Project's WBS in the form of an organizational chart. Although the figure looks like a traditional organizational chart, a project is really a process composed of many subprocesses. A process is series of steps that results in some outcome such as a deliverable. **Project processes** typically cluster into **project phases**. Projects, for example, have a **beginning phase** in which planning takes place and resources are gathered, a **middle phase** in which those resources are used to produce products and services, and an **ending phase** in which those products and services are delivered to the client and the project is closed down. Quite often, these three project phases can be broken down into several of their own subphases. Linda's project, for example, has an early "educational phase" in which each organizational area learns about the certification policies and procedures relevant to it. This leads to a "policies and procedures development phase" in which each area develops the policies and procedures it will use to comply with state requirements and prepare for certification visits. Project schedules help make these phases much more apparent and are covered in the next chapter.

This process perspective on project work also affects how tasks are best assigned. Because process tasks build on one another, it is generally best to use the same human resources throughout the process and, if appropriate, from one phase to another. By doing so, the project takes advantage of the learning curve that accompanies every project task. Those working on later tasks in a project build on their work earlier in the project. For example, in Figure 3.1, the Medical Care objective (4.0) requires that SOPs be developed (4.3.2) for three operational areas including Planning (4.3.2.1), Acute Care (4.3.2.2), and Chronic Care (4.3.2.3). It may well be that the same one or two project members should work on all three tasks to take advantage of learning as they develop SOPs in each one of them. Later in the project, these same members are likely to be well suited to play important roles in implementing those SOPs as well.

Breaking the project down into related processes also can help in the proper assignment of leadership positions within the project. The project leader, of course, is responsible for the entire project and has final authority over it. The project leader, however, may well delegate parts of the project to **project leads**, who have authority and direct control over the production and delivery of outputs for their project areas. In Linda's Compliance Project, for example, the division heads of each organizational division may be considered for project lead roles in each of their organizational areas. They would be held accountable for getting their related project work done and given project authority to do so. As the project leader, Linda would likely assume direct control over project planning and project administration activities. As the chief administrator, she would likely lead work, as well, in her own organizational area of Administration (1.0).

Higher level project leads may, in turn, delegate some authority to other personnel working below them. As authority is delegated down, those higher in the WBS chain have authority over—and are accountable for—work done lower in the WBS chain. Taking a process view of the project, those leading higher level phases or processes have authority over—and are accountable for—work done in lower level subprocesses. This approach to grouping project work and project leadership helps achieve both unity of effort and unity of command. **Unity of effort** ensures that the work product fits with other products to produce project deliverables efficiently and effectively. **Unity of command** means that project members have only one immediate supervisor, and there is only one supervisor accountable for work under his or her purview. In addition, those supervisors are arranged in a coherent hierarchy of authority from the lowest to the highest levels.[5]

While breaking down and reassembling the WBS, project leaders need also to specify, break out, and assign project work to facilitate command and control. Project tasks or work packages should be broken down in such a way that a concrete deliverable (i.e., a product or service) is produced by it. As was discussed in the last chapter, the best task deliverables are SMART: specific, measurable, actionable, realistic, and time-specific. Deliverables also should be an outcome of a complete phase, process, or subprocess, so those responsible for its output have control over all relevant developmental parts. Although more than one person may be working on a particular project component, to achieve unity of command in the project structure, only one will be the project lead—the one accountable for getting the deliverable produced.[6] Finally, the time allowed for the delivery of a task's product needs careful consideration. It may well be, for example, that it will take a month or more for a task's deliverable to be produced. That timeline, however, can undermine command and control in more complex and larger projects. There is a tendency to put off or "back load" project work when it is given longer lead times. While back loading may well be due to simple procrastination, it is more often due to other competing demands for a team member's attention. We tend to respond to the greatest threat, and those threats tend to be work due tomorrow. Rather than wait (and hope) for a final product far down the line, it is generally best to break down that work to require concrete products in the interim that will combine to the ultimate deliverable needed. For example, rather than wait a month to receive SOPs for a manager's entire division of four departments, Linda might ask her managers to produce an SOP for each unit, each week. If more time is needed to produce each SOP, Linda might require interim reports and products (outlines, check-off sheets, etc.) to make sure the task is moving as expected. The trade-off to consider here is to make sure product is being produced while not oversupervising or micromanaging good staff.

To conclude, when a project leader has developed the WBS, he or she has taken a giant step toward developing an overall project plan. The WBS allows for the development of resource and cost estimates as well as estimates of how long each task will take. Arranging those tasks through the project's life cycle is the next big step to take. We turn to that task in the next chapter on project scheduling. Table 3.2 presents a list of questions project leaders can ask themselves as they move through the process of creating a WBS and the estimates of work that follows from it. Although not exhaustive, it can provide a check-off list of some key things to consider.

Table 3.2   Work Breakdown Structure Check-Off List

Developing a WBS can be an involved process, not to mention developing the estimates of the resources, costs, and time requirements that flow from it. Listed here are a few key questions leaders should ask themselves as they move through the process of breaking down project work and developing estimates from the breakdown. The questions are meant to encourage project leaders to think through the issues involved and are used as a point of departure rather than as a comprehensive listing.

- What are the major jobs that need to be done to complete the core deliverables of this project? What are the tasks that need to be done to finish those major jobs?
- What are the major jobs that need to be done to support the project? Are more planning tasks required? What administrative tasks will be needed? Administrative tasks to consider include project meetings with the team, clients, and others; interim reports; administrative requirements of the host organization; periodic project reviews; procedures for compliance and certification requirements; and the like.
- Have the project tasks been detailed enough for good estimates to be made about resource, cost, and time requirements?
- Have all outsourced jobs been accounted for? What contracting requirements are needed to ensure deliverables according to specification, on time, and on budget? Will special attention, time, and payments be needed from the team or project leader to ensure delivery? Have these been included in the WBS?
- What are the resource needs for each task in the WBS? Are there any special resources that need to be nailed down or contracted? Are there resources that will be delivered from internal suppliers? What activities or tasks need to be done to ensure delivery when they are needed? Consider integrating these into your WBS.

- What are the time requirements for each task? Consider whether you should require interim deliverables if the time for task completion is too long.
- What are the cost requirements for each task? Have these been figured into a project budget?
- How will the project be organized? Consider grouping project tasks according to a process-based flow. Who will lead and be assigned to the various tasks and requirements in the WBS? Consider task assignments along process-based lines. Assign one and only one person to be accountable for task deliverables and process output.
- Who should review the WBS and related estimates? Consider future senior team members who will be working on the project tasks. Consider project leaders who have led similar projects. Consider experts in the tasks or fields of work both external and internal to the organization. Consult your supervisor.

SUMMARY

The work breakdown structure (WBS) is the foundation for any project. It defines the scope of work that must be done to produce the deliverables and is the basis for developing bottom-up estimates of the resources, time, and budget needed for the project. It is the foundation, too, on which the project structure is built to facilitate command and control of the project.

Creating a WBS begins by focusing on the deliverables that satisfy the project's objectives and identifying the general jobs needed to achieve them. Those jobs, in turn, are broken down into the more specific tasks involved. This process of decomposition is followed until the full scope of project work is identified and sufficient detail is reached to actually produce the resource, time, and cost estimates needed for the project.

WBSs are composed of both core and support components. Core components are all those tasks necessary to produce the deliverables promised to a client, and they generally receive the most attention. Support tasks are those activities necessary to see the project through and are often neglected in a WBS. Two main support jobs are project planning and project administration. Because planning is done before core work on a project, it is often neglected as a cost item. When dealing with a client, however, planning can be done in phases of more and more detail with decision points appropriately scheduled and costs recovered. Administrative support includes activities like meetings, client and organizational reports, project reviews, and compliance checks. The fact that they are often seen as incidental to core project activities means they are often overlooked. Whether overlooked or not, however, someone will pay for them.

After the project has been broken down, estimates can be developed, and the tasks can be reassembled into a project structure. Project estimates generally focus on resources (human, equipment, and materials), time, and costs. Estimates are most often made by using actual costs of similar or analogous projects as a beginning base or by calculating itemized estimates from each project task from the bottom up. All such estimates are inherently risky, and adjustments need to be developed to help offset those risks.

The project structure is built on the foundation of the WBS. It is built by reassembling its tasks into a structure that facilitates a common, detailed understanding of project work, on the one hand, and command and control of the project, on the other. Because projects are processes, project work is best grouped together into those processes that yield identifiable products and services for the project. Project phases, basic processes within them, and subprocesses within those are grouped together so those working within them can develop an identifiable product or service from beginning to end. To facilitate command and control, leadership in the project should be structured to promote unity of command. In addition, the outputs of project tasks and subprocesses should be defined in SMART and concrete terms. Finally, not too much time should pass before a task or set of tasks produces an identifiable product for possible project review, even if that product is an interim piece of the eventual product or service to be produced.

REVIEW QUESTIONS

1. What is a WBS?
   a. What are core and support tasks in a WBS?
   b. Identify two important kinds of support tasks in any project. Why is it important to include them in a WBS?

2. Describe the roles played by a WBS in a project.

3. How is a WBS produced?

4. WBSs are used for a variety of project tasks. One is estimating project resource needs, time, and costs.
   a. What are the two basic ways of estimating resources, time, and costs?
   b. What are their relative advantages and disadvantages?

5. What are the basic resources that need to be estimated in a project?
   a. What are the important considerations for each?

6. What are the important considerations when estimating time requirements of the tasks in a WBS?

7. What are the important considerations when estimating costs in a project?

8. How is a WBS useful in developing the organizational structure of a project?

   a. Cover such issues as how work should be grouped together, the delegation of work to facilitate command and control within broad areas of the project, and the specification of task output to facilitate command and control over the task.

EXERCISE[7]

1. Work individually or as a team to develop a WBS.

   a. Focus on a project that is relevant to you or your team.

   b. Identify two or three major project deliverables (products or services) to be produced and delivered.

   c. Develop WBSs for each of these deliverables. Keep breaking down the work into more and more detailed tasks until you are satisfied you can estimate the resource and time needs for them.

   d. Identify the resources needed to accomplish the tasks you have specified.

   e. Estimate the time needs and cost requirements of a significant portion of the tasks you have identified in your WBS.

   f. Arrange the tasks of your WBS into an organizational structure for your project.

   g. Make sure the organizational structure facilitates the delegation of authority in the project. Keep in mind and include any organizational considerations due to project phases.

ENDNOTES

1. Project Management Institute. (2008). *A guide to the project management body of knowledge* (4th ed., p. 452). Newtown Square, PA: Author.

2. Although a traditional organizational structure is pictured in Figure 3.1, many project structures are different from a traditional structure.

3. There are a number of guidelines regarding just where to stop in the process of breaking work down. I prefer the commonsense rule presented in the text. Another is the "80 hour" rule where work is broken down to the point where no more than 80 hours is needed to produce a deliverable. One advantage to this rule

is that deliverables have a short timeline, which aids in monitoring the project's output. I prefer a more commonsense approach here as well—not too much and not too little supervision—as discussed more fully in a section to come.

4.   You probably noticed that every task in the WBS in Figure 3.1 has a number attached to it, and I refer to them often. Although such numbering is optional, it is so important that it should be mandatory. You can think of these numbers in a way similar to those used when writing an outline. Instead of using Roman numerals for headings (e.g., I, I a., II, II a., II a.1), we use a decimal system (e.g., 1.0, 1.1, 2.0, 2.1, 2.2.1).

When this numbering system is applied to a WBS, it coincides with the breakdown logic used to produce the WBS. Higher level jobs composed of many tasks have higher level numbers. The tasks that need to be done for those jobs are numbered accordingly as the work is broken down into smaller and smaller tasks. In Linda's WBS, the project objective of administrative operations passing inspection (Administration) is given the highest-level number—a 1.0. This, along with the other most basic project objectives (Physical Therapy, Food/Nutrition, and so on), represents the first major division of the project; and these major divisions are all given the highest level numbers (e.g., 2.0, 3.0). As work is broken down in each of these areas, they are numbered accordingly—1.1, 1.2, and 1.3 for the next level of detail in 1.0 Administration, for example; then 1.3.1, 1.3.2, and 1.3.3 for the level of detail after that; and so on.

Such a numbering system is quite useful in keeping track of everything in a project. First, we know which tasks belong to which project task chain. Anything starting with a 3, for example, belongs to the Food/Nutrition component of the project. Second, when personnel decisions are made, project workers assigned to one level of project work (e.g., 3.2.2) are often responsible for all project tasks at levels lower than that number (e.g., 3.2.2.1 to 3.2.2.9). Third, people reviewing the project can find components of the project more easily when looking for heading numbers than heading titles alone. Finally, when reporting on a project, heading numbers can be used to establish parallels between the project report and the project tasks covered in the report.

5.   Project and matrix organizations interfere with unity of command in projects, with project staff reporting to both the project leader or manager and another organizational manager (e.g., a department head or functional manager). Project leaders need to manage this inherent conflict of command and not make it worse in the project itself.

6.   An old management saying goes, "When more than one person is responsible for getting the work done, no one is responsible for getting the work done."

7.   If you have project management software, use it to do these tasks.

KEY TERMS

Analogous Estimating: estimating by looking at actual resource, time, and cost estimates of similar projects or project components and adapting them to the current project. Also referred to as *top-down estimating*. Compare with bottom-up estimating.

Beginning Phase: typically the phase in which planning takes place and resources are gathered.

Bottom-Up Estimating: estimating the resources, time, and/or costs of each task itself. These estimates are then combined for project components and the project as a whole.

Command and Control: the use of project authority to monitor and control the use of resources to achieve project objectives.

Core Tasks: all those tasks necessary to produce the products and services that will be delivered to the client; compare with support tasks.

Decomposition: the technical name for breaking down jobs into ever smaller tasks.

Ending Phase: typically the phase in which products and services are delivered to the client and the project is closed down.

Lag Time: the amount of time a task needs to "rest" after work has been done on it.

Middle Phase: typically the phase in which resources are used to produce products and services.

Project Administration: all support tasks associated with administrating the project.

Project Leads: members of the project team who have authority and direct control over the production and delivery of project outputs for different parts of the project.

Project Phase: a cluster of related project processes.

Project Planning: all those support tasks performed before actually running a project in order to prepare for its execution.

Project Process: a series of steps that results in some outcome such as a deliverable.

Project Structure: the decomposed tasks in a WBS reassembled in a way that helps with the assignment of project work and the command and control of the project.

Support Tasks: all those tasks necessary for conducting the project itself (principally planning and administration).

Top-Down Estimating: estimating by looking at actual resource, time, and cost estimates of similar projects or project components and adapting them to the current project. Also referred to as *analogous estimating*. Compare with bottom-up estimating.

Work Breakdown Structure (WBS): a deliverable-oriented grouping of project tasks that organizes and defines the work scope of the project, itemizing all the tasks that must be done to produce the project's deliverables.

Work Packages: a collection of related project tasks resulting in a deliverable.

4

Project Scheduling

INTRODUCTION

DR. HOWARD'S BIO-INFORMATICS PROJECT

"Be careful what you wish for." That saying kept running through Dr. Dan Howard's head as he looked at the project ahead of him. Dr. Howard, a professor at a large Eastern university, was awarded a $5 million, 5-year contract by the National Institutes of Health (NIH) to expand his award-winning work in bio-informatics. But it wasn't the bio-informatics research that bothered him now. It was the setup required before he could do the work! In his proposal to NIH, he allocated time and money to refurbish and convert a large facility at the university's research park into a fully functioning laboratory. Extensive modifications needed to be made on the structure itself, of course, but that was only the beginning. Equipment had to be purchased, delivered, set up, and tested. Supplies needed to be ordered and stored—some of them in special kinds of storage, and some with only a short shelf life. Special security had to be arranged as well—given the nature of his work—and the federal government would review security arrangements to make sure it was up to standard. He also had to hire and train a large contingent of administrative and laboratory staff to support the work of the lead scientists. And he had to do all this and more in just 4 months!

CHAPTER OVERVIEW

Although Dr. Howard's project might be in the category of "high science," the headache he faces here is common to many kinds of projects—how to arrange a lot of different jobs to come together smoothly through time. This chapter addresses that basic issue. Project work must be scheduled so that the different parts come together to produce whatever is needed at the right time. We begin our discussion of project scheduling by looking at different kinds of project schedules and the components that make them up. Next, we discuss how schedules are constructed, focusing on the construction of Gantt or bar charts. Finally, we explore some of the ways that project leaders use their schedules.

PROJECT SCHEDULES: TYPES AND COMPONENTS

The **project schedule** orders project tasks and events through time. It indicates when tasks should start and end and how long they should take, and it arranges them in a logical order. It is the principal tool project leaders use to keep track of a project: whether things are getting done on time, costs are being used according to budget, resources are being delivered as needed, and deliverables are being produced as promised. Schedules also help project leaders keep track of what tasks are coming up that may need attention and resources. At its heart, a project schedule is simply a list of when project tasks are to begin and end. Because some tasks must finish before other tasks can start, most project schedules tie these tasks together with **dependencies**—linkages that show how tasks are dependent on one another. As projects grow in complexity, their activities and dependencies grow into more and more detailed networks. As you can guess, all of this can get very complicated very quickly. As a result, a number of visual, mathematical, and computer tools have been developed that help project leaders organize and visualize the way project tasks must occur through time.

TYPES OF PROJECT SCHEDULES

Three of the most common scheduling techniques are the Gantt or bar chart, the Critical Path Method, and the Program Evaluation and Review Technique.

The Gantt or Bar Chart

If you count nonprofessionals, Gantt or bar charts are likely the most commonly used scheduling tool because they are fairly easy to learn and can be used in even quite complex projects. **Gantt charts** illustrate project tasks as bars and place them across the days of a calendar. The length of the bar represents how long the task should take to get done. The beginning of the bar is placed on the calendar date where the task should begin, and the end of the bar shows when the task should end. If one task (e.g., staff training) depends on another task ending (e.g., staff hiring), the beginning of the dependent task's bar is placed at the end of the first task's bar because of that dependency. Sometimes, Gantt charts show arrows between these bars to illustrate their dependency.

Figure 4.1 presents a simple Gantt chart for ordering supplies in Dr. Howard's Bio-Informatics Project.[1] Figure 4.2 shows how Gantt charts can handle even more complex projects like the Bio-Informatics Project facing Dr. Howard. We will come back to this Gantt chart several more times to illustrate a number of points in this chapter.

Gantt charts are very good tools to use when trying to visualize a project's tasks through time and communicate that information to the project team and others. They are the most commonly used scheduling tool among nonprofessionals. They are fairly easy to learn and, with modern project management software, can be used to help plan and control quite complex projects.

Figure 4.1   A Simple Bar Chart—Ordering Supplies in Dr. Howard's Bio-Informatics Project

NOTE: Figure 4.1 was generated using Microsoft Excel©.

The Critical Path Method (CPM)

A schedule of tasks can also be shown as a network of arrows and nodes. The arrows show task dependencies, and the nodes show where tasks intersect. Figure 4.3 shows a simple network diagram laying out a study Dr. Howard might conduct in his laboratory once it is set up. In this procedure, Dr. Howard has to spend some time setting up the study he will run. He then needs to do three experiments to compare with one another, each of which has two stages. Finally, he has to analyze the data he developed from them and write up the results in a project report. In the diagram shown in Figure 4.3, the study tasks are represented as nodes with information in them (i.e., the number of the task, the task name, and time needed to complete it). The arrows simply show the relationship between those tasks.[2]

The **Critical Path Method** (CPM) is a mathematical calculation that uses the time estimates for each task to develop the project's critical path, as shown by the double-line arrows in Figure 4.3. A project's **critical path** is that sequence of tasks that, together, will take longer than any other set of tasks to get the project done. Because the project cannot be done any earlier, the critical path determines the earliest end date for the project. Needless to say, this path will command a great deal of the project leader's attention, and we will return to it later. The CPM was created by the DuPont Corporation to aid in its chemical plant projects and has been shown to be very useful across a variety of complex projects. Appendix A discusses how a critical path is calculated using CPM.

The Program Evaluation and Review Technique (PERT)

The **Program Evaluation and Review Technique** (PERT) uses a network diagram similar to the CPM. It uses three different time estimates, however, for the completion of each task instead of just one: an optimistic time, a likely time, and a pessimistic time. Each task, then, has a probability distribution attached to its time estimate. Mathematical techniques like Monte Carlo simulations[3] can be used throughout the project to calculate the probabilities that the project as a whole—or subcomponents in it—will be completed as required. This technique was created for use in the development of the Polaris Missile Submarine. PERT is still used for very complex projects (e.g., those involving breakthrough technologies) in which time estimates are inherently more risky.

COMPONENTS OF PROJECT SCHEDULES

Project schedules have a number of components that make them up. Each component plays an important role in building an effective schedule.

Figure 4.2 A Gantt Chart Illustrating Dr. Howard's Bio-Informatics Project

ID	WBS	Task Name
1	1	**Physical Plant**
2	1.1	**Prep Plant**
3	1.1.1	Review/Rev Plans
4	1.1.2	Gut Existing Space
5	1.2	**Develop Infrastructure**
6	1.2.1	Framing
7	1.2.2	Electrical/Wiring
8	1.2.3	Plumbing
9	1.2.4	Dry wall
10	1.2.5	Finishing
11	1.3	Finish Plant
12	2	**Equipment**
13	2.1	**Lab equipment**
14	2.1.1	Review Plans
15	2.1.2	Select & Purchase
16	2.1.3	Deliver
17	2.1.4	Set up
18	2.1.5	Test
19	2.2	**Office Equipment**
20	2.2.1	Review needs
21	2.2.2	Select & Purchase
22	2.2.3	Deliver
23	2.2.4	Set up
24	2.3	Finish equipment set-up
25	3	**Personnel**
26	3.1	**Current lab & office staff**
27	3.1.1	Update personnel files
28	3.2	**New lab & office staff**
29	3.2.1	Review needs
30	3.2.2	Recruiting
31	3.2.3	Selecting
32	3.2.4	Training
33	3.3	Finish Personnel
34	4	**Security**
35	4.1	Review & vet vendors
36	4.2	Negotiate contracts
37	4.3	Orientation of personnel
38	4.4	Government review
39	4.5	Finish security set-up
40	5	**Supplies**
41	5.1	Review needs
42	5.2	Select vendors
43	5.3	Order non-perishables
44	5.4	Deliver
45	5.5	Store
46	5.6	Finish Supplies
47	6	Finish lab set up

Project: Dr. Howard's Gantt chart

Task   Critical Task   Milestone ◆   Summary

Page 1

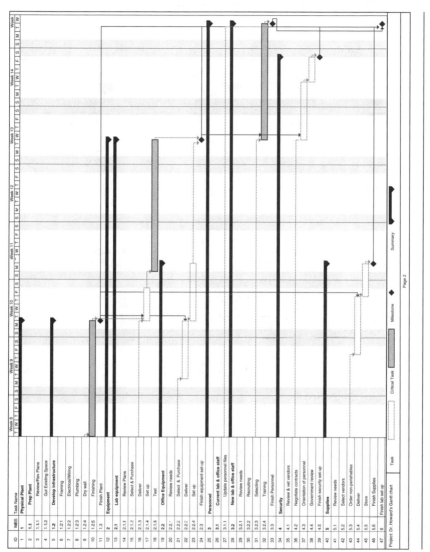

NOTE: Figure 4.2 was generated using Microsoft Project©. WBS = Work breakdown structure.

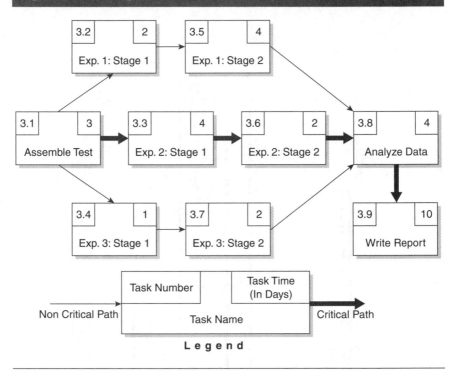

Figure 4.3 A Simple Project Network Diagram—Dr. Howard's Study

NOTE: Exp. = experiment.

Activities or Project Tasks

An **activity** is anything in a project that will require time to complete and usually money and other resources as well. Most often, activities are team tasks needed to produce project deliverables as determined by the project's work breakdown structure (WBS). Sometimes, however, project activities include tasks that lie outside what the project team is doing. For example, your boss, bank, or some regulator may have to approve something in your project before it can move forward. You want to make sure you include these kinds of external activities in your WBS and schedule as well.

Dependencies

Dependencies occur when one task is dependent on another task in some way. The most common form is the **finish-to-start dependency,** in which one or more tasks must finish before one or more tasks can begin. In Dr. Howard's project (Figure 4.2), for example, he must finish selecting new laboratory personnel (3.2.3) before their training (3.2.4) can start. Three other less common dependencies are "start-to-start," "finish-to-finish," and "start-to-finish" dependencies. In a **start-to-start dependency**, two or more tasks must start at the same time. When Dr. Howard is actually conducting experiments, for example, he may have to start two or more of them at the same time to get valid results. In a **finish-to-finish dependency**, two or more tasks must finish at the same time. Although the delivery of equipment might begin at any time for Dr. Howard's lab, for example, that activity must finish (i.e., be finally delivered to the lab) when the lab itself is finished so it can be moved in. Finally, a **start-to-finish dependency** signals that one or more tasks must start for one or more tasks to be finished.

Lag and Lead Times

Lag and lead times affect task dependencies in terms of the amount of time that must pass in one task before another task can be related to it. **Lag time** is the amount of time that must pass after work has been done on a task before work can start on a dependent, following, or succeeding task. Concrete must cure for a while, for example, before anything can be built on it. Dr. Howard's study in Figure 4.3 may show another example of lag time. Each of the three experiments may require growing bacteria in petri dishes. It may take only half a day to set up the growth, but the remaining time in Stage 1 for each experiment may be needed for the growth to reach maturity for that particular line of bacteria.

Lead time means something very specific in project schedules. It means that a following dependent task can begin before a beginning or preceding task has completely finished—it can "lead" the finish of the beginning task. In the construction of Dr. Howard's lab (Figure 4.2), for example, the wiring (1.2.2) and plumbing (1.2.3) can begin before all the walls are put up (Framing, 1.2.1). If the walls take 15 days to complete, the wiring and plumbing might begin when two thirds of the walls are completed, thereby leading the completion by 5 days.

Milestones

Milestones are important events in the life of a project but consume no time or resources. They are usually added to a project schedule to signal when some component of the project should have been completed. In Dr. Howard's project shown in Figure 4.2, for example, every major project component (e.g., [1] Physical Plant, [2] Equipment) has a "finish" scheduled as a milestone (e.g., 1.3, 2.3, 3.3). Often, milestones require some report or other deliverable to the client or to another stakeholder. If so, then it is important to remember that this kind of milestone must be preceded by activities that produce whatever is needed for the milestone and that they be included in the work breakdown structure, schedule, cost estimates, and the like.

The Project Network

Because a project ultimately depends on all project tasks being done at some point, all the project's activities and milestones will eventually be tied together in a complex arrangement of project tasks, known as the **project network**. Figure 4.3 of Dr. Howard's study shows a network as it is commonly conceived. All tasks are connected and eventually lead to the project's final goal. The Gantt chart in Figure 4.2 shows the bio-informatics project network, but rather than nodes and arrows, the Gantt chart uses bars and arrows to represent how the tasks connect to each other and eventually lead to the project's completion.

The Critical Path

Every project has a **critical path**—a sequence of tasks that will take longer to do than any other sequence of tasks. The project's critical path determines the earliest date the project can be completed. Because any change in the critical path affects the whole project, it commands a great deal of attention from project leaders. In planning, most risk assessments about the time it will take to do a task will be done along this path. If a leader wants to shorten the project completion date, he or she will work with the tasks scheduled along this path. While the project is being conducted, project leaders may take resources from an activity off the critical path and give them to an activity that is on the critical path to keep the project on schedule or to shorten the overall project—an activity known as "**crashing**."

The double-line arrows show the critical path in Dr. Howard's study in Figure 4.3. The critical path can also be shown in Gantt charts. In Figure 4.2, for example, the critical path is indicated by the solid gray bars in the diagram connected to each other with arrows—those are the tasks that make up the critical path. They must start and end as scheduled for the project to finish on time.

Slack or Float

Tasks that lie off the critical path have **slack** (also known as **float**). Those tasks can begin and finish later than scheduled without pushing back the completion time for the project as a whole. For example, take a look at the "Office Equipment" (2.2) task of selecting and purchasing of equipment (2.2.2) in the Gantt chart in Figure 4.2. It is scheduled to begin on the 2nd day of the project and will be finished in the following week. Delivery (2.2.3) of the equipment, however, cannot begin until near the completion date of laboratory construction some 8 weeks later. Selection and purchasing of office equipment, then, has a fair amount of slack. Dr. Howard may choose to put off that task until later and use its personnel for other, more pressing, project work.

HOW TO DEVELOP A PROJECT SCHEDULE: FOCUS—GANTT CHARTS

We will focus on developing Gantt charts because they tend to be the most useful for most projects. Before we begin, however, it would be a good idea to look at the Gantt chart of Dr. Howard's project in Figure 4.2. Although it might seem complicated at first, there are really just three basic parts to it. The first is the work breakdown structure in the left-hand column. This was produced using the approach to breaking down project work covered in Chapter 3. The work in Dr. Howard's project is clustered into five major components: (1) Physical Plant, (2) Equipment, (3) Personnel, and so on. Each of those project components contains all the project activities or tasks relevant to them. All these components and tasks are numbered in "outline form." The largest numbers are given to the largest project components (e.g., 1 Physical Plant). The smallest numbers within each component represent individual activities or tasks. Any numbers in between show how large project components are broken down into smaller project components (e.g., 1.1 Prep Plant and 1.2 Develop Infrastructure).

The second major part of a Gantt chart is the **project calendar**. The days of the calendar are laid out across the top of the chart, and those days create columns down the rest of the chart. In Dr. Howard's Gantt chart, the days are clustered by week, and actual dates are often given for the project calendar. That calendar shows Saturdays and Sundays, as well as the days of the normal workweek. I like to include them to help visually keep track of the weeks in a project. Most often, however, they are not counted as project work time.

The final part of the Gantt chart is the information that lies out across the project calendar. The most important information is given in the **task bars** that represent each project task. The length of each task bar is the time it should take to do the task. Where the bar is placed on the calendar indicates when the task should start and end. Those bars are also arranged in terms of their dependency on one another. If one task cannot begin until another task is done, its task bar is placed after that preceding task. That dependency is also shown in Dr. Howard's Gantt chart with arrows connecting the bars.

There are other, **summary bars** as well. They "summarize" how long related clusters of project tasks should take and when each task cluster should begin and end. Finally, you can see milestones on Dr. Howard's Gantt chart represented by diamonds. They indicate important dates in the project—usually when some larger component of project work should be done. Of course, many other kinds of information can be placed on the Gantt chart, but this is sufficient for most modest projects.

There are five basic steps to producing Gantt charts like Dr. Howard's. First, create a work breakdown structure in outline form. Second, review the times needed to complete each task. Third, determine the dependency between those tasks—what needs to be done first, second, third, and the like, so that other tasks can follow and build on the initial ones. Fourth, construct the project network of tasks across the project's calendar. Fifth, determine the project's critical path.

Create a Work Breakdown Structure in Outline Form

As covered in Chapter 3, the WBS identifies the tasks that need to be done in a project. To create a Gantt chart, those tasks need to be arranged in outline form. The outline form is created to help keep similar, related tasks together. Dr. Howard's Gantt chart in Figure 4.2 provides a good example of a WBS in outline form in the chart's far left columns.

Review Time Estimates

You may recall that when a WBS is developed, time estimates are made for how long the individual tasks will take to complete. Those estimates should be reviewed prior to the schedule's construction, and they should include such considerations as required lag time.[4] As was suggested in Chapter 3, it is a good idea to think about optimistic and pessimistic time estimates as well as your "best guess." The time risks of a project are a major threat to getting the project done on time and on budget and deserve extra attention.

Determine Task Dependencies

The next step to take is to determine how project tasks relate to one another—their dependencies. The most common dependency is the finish-to-start dependency—one task must finish before another can start.

It is helpful to start this task by looking within project job categories first. For example, in Dr. Howard's project in Figure 4.2, attention might be given to the Physical Plant first and to its related tasks. It is because these tasks *are* related that dependencies are likely to occur among them. In a similar manner, a first pass looking for dependencies would progress through all the other major project components.

Next, it is a good idea to step back a bit and consider how major project categories relate to one another. "Developing the Physical Plant" in the Dr. Howard's project, for example, is necessary before most other activities can be done within the finished laboratory. The last task of construction, then, needs to precede all those other dependent activities.

CONSTRUCT THE NETWORK OF PROJECT ACTIVITIES

The next step is to construct the schedule network itself. In Gantt charts, each task in the work breakdown outline is given its own row, and the tasks are clustered into project components of related activities. Recall that the columns to the right of the task listing represent time intervals in a project calendar—quite often, days of the week.

Initially, focus is given to individual project tasks. Task bars are drawn so that their length represents how long they will take to get done. Then they are placed on the calendar at the point of their earliest start date. As you place or draw the task bars across the project calendar, you need to keep in mind the dependencies between tasks—not starting a task, for example, before another, dependent task is finished.

When the bars for all project tasks have been placed on the calendar, higher order "summary bars" can be drawn to completely encompass the lower order tasks that make them up. These summary bars visually summarize and unite the project work beneath them into their higher order project components.

Once all the bars are placed on the project calendar, their dependencies can be shown by drawing arrows from the end of a preceding task to the beginning of a successor task that depends on it. In Gantt charts, the arrow goes straight across the row of the preceding task before it moves down to connect with its successor task. The length of the arrow indicates the preceding task's slack or float, as shown in Dr. Howard's project in Figure 4.2.[5]

DETERMINE THE CRITICAL PATH

Finding a project's critical path is rather straightforward, but the calculations involved can become quite challenging in complex projects. Project management software provides the best solution to this task. Nevertheless, project leaders should have a basic understanding of the process involved.

Recall that the critical path is the longest sequence of activities from the beginning of a project to its end. Because, eventually, all activities are connected to both the beginning and the end of the project, one path of project tasks will come up as the longest. The key to finding the critical path, then, is to trace the various paths of dependent activities in a project from its beginning to its end, always making sure to focus on the path that is taking the longest time to complete. To do so, keep adding the time it takes to do a task to the dependent task that comes next. Whenever two or more paths come together, choose the path with the longest time and begin tracing the next sequence of tasks from it. Eventually, this process ends with the last project task sequence. This process is known as a **"forward pass"** because you start at the beginning of the project, adding task times until you reach the end, and it results in two outcomes. The first is the amount of time it will take to finish the project—the sum of the longest sequence of task times. The second outcome is the identification of the longest sequence of tasks itself—the critical path. Any change in time for any of those tasks will affect the finish date of the project.

In critical path calculations, a **"backward pass"** is usually done as well. Beginning with the last task's finish date, subtract task times along task sequences. Doing so will indicate the amount of slack time between dependent tasks—none for those on the critical path and various amounts of slack for those tasks off the critical path. A more detailed description of the CPM is beyond the scope of this chapter, but Appendix A, "Calculating the Critical Path Using the Critical Path Method," demonstrates both the forward and backward pass and the calculations that result from them.

USING THE OUTPUT
OF A PROJECT SCHEDULE

The project's work schedule plays a variety of roles for the project leader. These roles include helping visualize the project as a whole, revising the project's estimates, and making project adjustments. Finally, because the schedule arranges project tasks through time, it allows project leaders to command, control, and coordinate resource use and outcomes of the project.

VISUALIZING THE PROJECT AS A WHOLE

One of the most important benefits of the project schedule is that it provides a "whole picture" of the project. As we said in Chapter 3, the WBS provides a list of all the tasks, and if graphed appropriately, it can provide a picture of the project's structure as well (e.g., recall the Compliance Project graphed in Figure 3.1). The project schedule, however, is the only tool that arranges the project's tasks through time. At first glance, the Gantt chart of Dr. Howard's Bio-Informatics Project in Figure 4.2 might seem a bit confusing. Project leaders, staff, and others quickly learn to read such schedules, however, like orchestra leaders and musicians read music. In fact, project schedules are designed, in part, to help project stakeholders see the phases and dependencies within a project and to communicate with one another.

Project Phases

As one looks past the individual tasks to see the outlines of the project as a whole, the phases of the project begin to emerge. All projects are composed of tasks done through time, and clusters of them often have to be done before other clusters. These task clusters form the various phases and subcomponents of a project. Different resources are likely to be needed in different phases, and each phase is likely to require different deliverables for the project as a whole. Who leads what activities may also change across project phases and project task clusters.

Project Dependencies

Another pattern that emerges from a project schedule is its network of task dependencies. These dependencies are shown as task "strings" through the project. The most commanding of these strings is the critical path—that sequence of tasks that determines the earliest completion date of the project. Possible project errors are riskier along this path because even a small problem here can affect the whole project. Tasks that lie off the critical path—although connected—are less critical to the timing of the project. Problems that occur with those tasks provide less risk to the project because their start and end dates are not as constrained—they have more slack. This slack in noncritical tasks, in turn, provides "wiggle room" for the project and its leader. Project schedules help make these task dependencies and risks very clear.

Communication to Stakeholders

Because the project schedule provides a graphical arrangement of all project tasks through time, it has the unique ability to provide both a broad understanding of the project as well as a more detailed calculation of the work required. As such, it makes for an excellent communication device for all stakeholders. The pace and timing of the project, for example, can be more easily communicated to clients. The most appropriate times for decision points, milestones, project reports, transfers of funds, and interim deliverables can be quickly and clearly communicated to clients with a project schedule. The project schedule is also useful in communicating with the host organization. When funds must flow to the project, when resources will be required, when updates make the most sense, and similar issues are all more clearly communicated with the help of project schedules. Those working on the project also use the schedule as a principal aid in communicating with each other. Different project team members can see very clearly when their work must begin and end. They can also have a clear picture of the project as a whole in addition to their part of it. This allows them to see where their work fits in with the work of others and how it will be used. Finally, internal and external suppliers can use the project schedule to see when their input is needed to make sure the right resources get to the right people at the right time.

REVISION OF PLANNING ASSUMPTIONS AND ESTIMATES FOR THE PROJECT PLAN

When a schedule is first produced, it aids in revising assumptions and estimates from the project's earlier planning stage. Those assumptions and estimates were made when the WBS was first developed—before consideration was given to how the tasks are connected to each other through time. When the schedule is developed and dependencies are determined, those estimates may need revision. Team members responsible for project components may notice tasks that need to be added or others that are not needed at all. Project staff may also be able to provide more input into resource needs, personnel, time estimates, and dependencies between tasks when studying the schedule.

Internal and external resource suppliers can use the schedule to confirm availability of resources or discuss adjustments that need to be made. Project leaders themselves may see things that they missed earlier in the planning phase. All changes, of course, have effects across the project. Because the schedule indicates what task sequences are most critical for getting the project done (e.g., those on the critical or near-critical paths[6]), particular attention can be given to the risk assessments of those tasks in particular.

Another assumption that needs to be checked is the level of resource use at any particular time in the project. When developing the initial WBS, resources are committed to tasks without regard to when they are to be used. When those tasks are scheduled at specific times, some resources may become overcommitted. Logistical problems may arise in the scheduling of equipment use and the flow of material. Personnel may also be overcommitted. For example, some team members may be scheduled to work more than 40 hours per week once tasks are arranged across time. Noncritical tasks with slack, then, can be moved forward or backward on the schedule to redistribute personnel and/or resources to help address this problem.

Project leaders typically spend a great deal of time revising and modifying the initial schedule to address issues and problems such as these. In truth, addressing all these matters can be quite frustrating. Project leaders need to keep in mind, however, that these issues are better confronted in the earlier planning stages rather than later on when they will cost more time and money and will provide even more frustration.

MAKING ADJUSTMENTS TO THE PLAN THROUGHOUT THE PROJECT

Because projects are unique endeavors, leaders often find that adjustments need to be made while the project is under way to keep it on schedule and on budget. Project schedules allow project leaders to see the effects of any such adjustments they make. These effects can be seen even more clearly when using project management software. When resources are moved and times adjusted, the program can instantaneously update the resource use listings and the schedule, showing any changes in the critical path.

Project leaders quite often take resources from activities off the critical path and commit them to tasks on the critical path to help them reduce project risk, shorten project time, or keep the project on schedule if it is falling behind. If the project budget is in trouble, project leaders tend to look to tasks off the critical path for cutbacks. Although this is an acceptable approach to making needed adjustments, there are a number of problems that can emerge if the project leader is not careful.

First, resource shifts may lengthen other project tasks to the extent that a new critical path is developed. If a noncritical activity has only one day of slack, for example, shifting resources from it may lengthen its time horizon beyond that one day, making it critical (e.g., the plumbing task [1.2.3] in Figure 4.2 becomes critical with the addition of a single day and pushes the whole project back if it takes any longer). For these reasons, project leaders often conduct "**sensitivity analyses**" on their critical paths. One approach is to shorten time estimates of activities on the critical path to see if other task sequences become critical. Another approach is to lengthen estimates of tasks off the critical path to see if their task sequences then become critical. If the sensitivity analysis reveals any task sequences that have the potential of becoming critical, note should be made of them. Project leaders will need to pay as much attention to these **near-critical tasks** as they do to tasks along the critical path.

A second problem that can emerge when making adjustments in the middle of a project is an overuse of resources. It is not unusual, for example, that a member of the project team is working on several project tasks or both project and nonproject tasks at the same time. Looking at the work he or she is doing on only one project task can lead to the mistaken notion that the member can work elsewhere, resulting in overload. The same kind of overloading problem can arise with equipment and other resources. Careful tracking of scheduled resource use can help address this risk.[7]

A final problem emerges with what might be called "resource mathematics." Doubling the number of people working on a task, for example, rarely cuts task time in half. This is the case for at least two reasons. One is that increasing the number of personnel creates process loss. Problems with coordination, information sharing, "free riding," and the like tend to increase with more personnel. Another reason is that resources are often not smoothly interchangeable. It takes time to get up to speed, for example, when working on a new job. In addition, the knowledge, skills, and abilities of the new personnel may not fit as well to the new job's requirements.

COMMAND AND CONTROL

Still another key benefit of the project schedule is its use as a tool for project control. As a project network moves through time, a variety of project tasks must be done and resources used. Schedules help leaders manage those activities by clearly showing what tasks are currently in progress, who is working on them, and how close they should be to completion. Depending on the task's slack, project leaders know how much attention should be given to its on-time completion. As resources are used by the project, leaders can keep track and compare them to what was budgeted to keep control of project costs. (One tool used for cost control making use of the schedule is Earned Value Analysis and is discussed in Appendix B.)

Schedules also let project leaders look into the near- and farther term futures of their projects. Armed with the knowledge of what will be required, leaders can ensure resources are available; adjust schedules and tasks; and anticipate, analyze, and address potential problems. Table 4.1 presents a list of questions project leaders can ask themselves as they move through the process of creating a schedule. Although not exhaustive, it can provide a check-off list of some key things to consider.

Table 4.1   Schedule Check-Off List

Depending on its complexity, a schedule can be a fairly straightforward or difficult tool to construct. Without a schedule, though, leaders cannot manage their projects. Listed here are a few key questions leaders should ask themselves as they move through the process of constructing a schedule. The questions are meant to be used as a point of departure, to help encourage project leaders to think through the issues involved in creating a project schedule. Leaders should add other questions as they see fit. The assumption made here is that the schedule will be in the form of a Gantt chart and that a critical path will be developed.

- Have all the core and support activities been included in the schedule? Have they been grouped together along work process lines and arranged appropriately in an outline form?
- Have all other scheduled work tasks been included? Consider the initiation and delivery of outsourced work. Consider regulatory reviews if required.
- Have task time estimates been reviewed and confirmed? Have they been properly represented in the schedule?
- Have lag times been incorporated into those tasks that require them? Consider any task that needs time to rest or mature after active work has finished.
- Have all task dependencies been included and reviewed in the schedule?
- Can some dependent tasks incorporate lead time? Is it possible for a dependent task to begin before its preceding task is complete?
- Have project milestones been placed appropriately in the project schedule? Consider locating them at times of project component reviews and completions. Will milestones require reviews or reports? If so, schedule the required tasks and include them in the WBS, budget, and related planning documents.
- Has a critical path been determined? Have near-critical tasks been identified?
- Has task slack of noncritical project tasks been determined?
- Does the visual layout of the project schedule make sense? Does the schedule communicate to the leader and to others the overall flow of the project in ways that will make sense to them? Consider whether work processes are clustered together in ways that make sense to those who work in and interact within them. Consider whether project phases make sense. Consider project dependencies between large project components as well as specific work tasks.
- Have resource requirements been arranged according to their scheduled use? Is any resource overcommitted or undercommitted? Consider the workweeks and workloads of all project personnel. Consider the logistical requirements of all equipment and materials needed. Have arrangements been scheduled for their on-time delivery? Have any project task requirements of those arrangements been scheduled?
- Has the project budget been arranged in accordance with the project schedule of resource use and revenue requirements? How easy is it to determine whether the project is on budget at any particular time during the project?

SUMMARY

Project schedules are basic and invaluable tools for project planning and management. At its most basic, a project schedule is simply an arrangement of project tasks across time. Different kinds of schedules help project leaders build on this fundamental notion. Gantt or bar charts use bars to represent project activities, with the length of the bar representing the length of the activity. These bars are placed on a project calendar to show start and end times at certain dates. The Critical Path Method (CPM) is a tool that helps project leaders determine a project's critical path in a project's task network and the slack of those tasks that do not lie on that path. The Program Evaluation and Review Technique (PERT) accounts for time risks in projects by incorporating optimistic and pessimistic time estimates for tasks in addition to their likely completion times.

Project schedules have a number of components in common. All have project activities or tasks that are scheduled to begin and end at certain times. Most have milestones that represent important events in the life of a project. Whether shown on a schedule or not, project tasks are tied together by their dependencies—one must end, for example, before another can begin. Eventually, all project tasks are linked in some fashion, and those linkages can be represented in a project network of task dependencies shown by arrows connecting dependent tasks. One particular sequence of dependent tasks represents the critical path of a project—that sequence of tasks determines the earliest date the project can end. The dependent tasks on the critical path must begin and end no later than scheduled or the project gets pushed back. All other tasks have some degree of float or slack—their start and finish times can vary to some extent without the project completion date being affected.

Project schedules are constructed from the activities in the WBS, their time estimates, and their dependencies on one another. The first step in developing a Gantt chart is to break down the project's work and arrange it in outline form on a spreadsheet. The rows of the spreadsheet will be dedicated to the project's tasks and the columns to the project calendar—most often representing days. Second, estimations of the time to complete each task are made and reviewed. Third, dependencies between tasks are determined. Fourth, the Gantt chart is built by constructing and placing bars for each activity on the project calendar. The length of each bar is constructed to be as long as the time estimate of the task. It is placed where the task is to begin on the project calendar. Dependent tasks do not begin until their predecessor tasks are completed as required. Gantt charts often connect their bars with arrows showing task dependencies as well.

A project schedule serves a variety of purposes. One is that it helps the project leader to visualize the project as a whole with its various phases and dependencies. It also helps other stakeholders to visualize the project and serves as an excellent communication device to the project's clients, its host organization, and others. Another use of the project schedule is to help in the revision of project assumptions and estimates. Once it is seen as a whole, various stakeholders can review the tasks, assumptions, and estimates to assess any problems, additions, or opportunities for the project. The project schedule also is critical in project revisions and adjustments. From initial planning to the ending of a project, leaders are called on to make adjustments of one sort or another. The project schedule helps guide such adjustments by making clear how they affect other tasks, resources, and project time. Finally, project schedules play an important role in command and control of the project. They help project leaders focus their attention on critical tasks and resources as the project moves forward and allow them to keep track of how the project is progressing and using its available resources.

REVIEW QUESTIONS

1. What is a project schedule?

2. Describe the three kinds of scheduling techniques covered in this chapter.

3. What are the components of project schedules covered in this chapter?

4. Define and give examples of dependent tasks.

5. Define and give examples of tasks with lag and lead times.

6. Define and give examples of tasks that have float or slack in relation to other tasks.

7. What is a project's critical path? What role does the critical path play in project management?

8. Describe the process of developing a project schedule. Use either the Gantt chart or the CPM technique in your discussion.

9. What are the ways project schedules are used in projects?

EXERCISE

1. Work individually or as a team to develop a project schedule. In this exercise, you will build a Gantt chart.[8]

    a. Focus on a project that is relevant to you or your team.

    b. Develop a WBS for a significant portion of your project (if you developed a WBS for Chapter 3, you can use it for this exercise).

c. Display the WBS in outline form on sheets of graph paper (if you are using project management software, display the tasks in it). Leave a few rows above your WBS outline.

d. On a row above the beginning of the WBS, start numbering columns to the left of the WBS. These columns will represent the days of your project from Day 1 to the final day.

e. Estimate the time required to complete each task.

f. Determine any dependencies between tasks.

g. Draw a line to the left of each task representing the time it will take to accomplish. Begin with the first tasks that can be done. Start dependent tasks where required preceding tasks have ended.

h. Continue building your Gantt chart, keeping in mind dependencies and lag times.

i. When you are done, evaluate the project network you have created. Identify needs for required modification and opportunities to shorten the schedule.

ENDNOTES

1. This sequence of tasks is shown without regard to the other tasks in the larger project shown in Figure 4.2.

2. This is called an activity-on-node diagram because the activity or task is displayed in the nodes of the network. There are also activity-on-arrow diagrams, in which the task is labeled on the arrow instead of in the node. These are used far less frequently.

3. Monte Carlo simulation is named after Monte Carlo gambling wheels. Each "spin of the wheel" assumes a particular start and end date for project tasks. Computers can spin the wheel thousands of times very quickly and calculate the likely distribution of project times between the beginning and end of a project or any sequence of tasks within it. This is beyond the scope of this book, however.

4. I like to include lag time for such things as vendor delivery of purchases, inspectors showing up once notified, and the like.

5. When doing this by hand, arrows are usually optional. In more complex projects, they add valuable visual information and are easily constructed with project management software. In fact, modern project management software can make the process of developing project schedules a fairly easy one. Microsoft Project©, for example, facilitates constructing a work breakdown structure, estimating activity times, drawing bars, linking them with arrows, and placing them on a project calendar all at the same time when developing a Gantt chart. The Gantt chart of the Bio-Informatics Project in Figure 4.2, for example, is based on the output of Microsoft Project©.

6. A near-critical path is a sequence of tasks that are close to becoming critical. More attention is given to this issue shortly.

7. Project management software can help reduce this risk by keeping track of resource use at any point in time.

8. This exercise is designed to produce a Gantt chart. The exercise assumes that the reader is not using project management software. If the reader is using project software, disregard references to using graph paper and so forth. Instead of graph paper, spreadsheet programs can be used if project management software is unavailable.

KEY TERMS

Activity: anything in a project that will take time to complete and usually money and other resources as well. Most commonly activities are project team tasks, but outside activities or tasks are included as well.

Backward Pass: a process for calculating slack or float in a project based on calculations made on a forward pass through the project. See Appendix A for more detail.

Crashing: when project leaders take resources from an activity off the critical path and give them to an activity on the critical path to keep the project on schedule or to shorten the overall project.

Critical Path: that sequence of tasks that, together, will take longer than any other set of tasks to get the project done. The critical path determines how long a project will take.

Critical Path Method (CPM): a method for determining a project's critical path.

Dependencies: a task relationship that occurs when one task is dependent on another task in some way.

Finish-to-Finish Dependency: a task dependency in which two or more tasks must finish at the same time.

Finish-to-Start Dependency: a task dependency in which one or more tasks must finish before one or more tasks can begin.

Float: the amount of time that a noncritical task can wait to begin or finish without pushing back the completion time for the project as a whole. Also known as "slack."

Forward Pass: a process for determining a project's critical path. See Appendix A for more detail.

Gantt Charts: a type of project schedule that illustrates project tasks as bars and places them across the days of a calendar. The length of the bar indicates the time it should take for the task to be done.

Lag Time: the amount of time that must pass after work has been done on a task before work can start on a dependent, succeeding task.

Lead Time: the amount of time that a succeeding dependent task can begin before a preceding task has completely finished.

Milestones: important events in the life of a project that consume no time or resources. They often signal the completion of important project work.

Near-Critical Tasks: any task sequences that have the potential of becoming critical if small time adjustments are made to the tasks.

Program Evaluation and Review Technique (PERT): a network diagram that uses three different time estimates for each task or activity—an optimistic time, a likely time, and a pessimistic time for its completion.

Project Calendar: the calendar for starting and completing tasks in a project. In Gantt charts, the project calendar is represented by dates across the top of the chart, which are then used to divide the chart into columns. Task bars and other time-relevant information are then placed across those time columns.

Project Network: a complex arrangement of project tasks in which all tasks are connected by arrows and eventually lead to the project's final goal.

Project Schedule: orders project tasks and events through time. It indicates when tasks should start and end and how long they should take, and it arranges them in a logical order.

Sensitivity Analyses of the Critical Path: a method to determine if there are any near-critical paths in a project. Time is shortened on the critical path or lengthened on noncritical paths to see if other paths become critical.

Slack: the amount of time that a noncritical task can wait to begin or finish without pushing back the completion time for the project as a whole. Also known as "float."

Start-to-Finish Dependency: a task dependency in which one or more tasks must start for one or more tasks to be finished.

Start-to-Start Dependency: a task dependency in which two or more tasks must start at the same time.

Summary Bars: bars on a Gantt chart that summarize the length of time to complete a group of related tasks.

Task Bar: bar on a Gantt chart the length of which represents the time estimated to do the task.

5

Managing Project Risk

INTRODUCTION

THE CRIME TRACKING PROJECT

"Can it get any worse?" This was the recurring thought of Police Chief David Sessions as he looked back over a week of very bad news. Chief Sessions was leading a project to integrate police information about crimes and suspects across four jurisdictions of neighboring cities. Criminals often cross city and county lines, and the ability to keep track of them as they do has become a powerful tool for police departments. Teaming with the police chiefs of the other three police departments, Chief Sessions was able to land a large 2-year federal grant to help fund this project. The main objectives of the project were to create the data linkages between the departments and to establish standard operating procedures for effectively keeping track of and responding to crime across city lines.

Chief Sessions, along with the other police chiefs, developed the plans for the project by researching similar projects undertaken successfully in other communities and adapting those plans to the needs of their four cities.

Developing those plans and getting them approved took an entire year of working with the various police departments, mayors, city managers, city councils, and other significant stakeholders.

Six months into the project, Chief Sessions was running into all kinds of unanticipated problems that had come to a head this week. For one, the computer systems in all the police departments had major difficulties communicating with each other. Plus, a trial run on how information could be used by patrol officers found that the officers couldn't get the information they needed. One likely reason was inadequate training. The other was problems with the on-board computers' software. The vendor of the computers, Patrol Computers, had cut back on the training because the computers were supposedly so "user-friendly" that a lot of training was not necessary. Early testing of the computers had also revealed problems, but Patrol Computers had not fixed them. On top of this, Patrol Computers filed for bankruptcy protection this week.

In another development, a city manager who was a major supporter of the project recently retired. This was not really a surprise, but the new city manager wanted a full review of the project, possibly leading to changes that "more adequately address her city's needs." Chief Sessions also learned this week that federal funding for the project had to be cut for the next funding period and, likely, reduced for the overall project. The final straw was a cease-and-desist order from a state regulator for failing to follow mandated procedures for cross-jurisdictional work. "Can it get any worse?" the chief kept thinking. Unfortunately, the answer to that question may, in fact, be "yes."

CHAPTER OVERVIEW

As we have discussed, projects produce new and unique products and services. They often do so using new people, methods, and materials. In addition to all this "newness," they often cost a lot of money and take up a lot of time, and others often depend on their outcomes a great deal. All this adds up to a lot of potential risk for a project. Project leaders, then, need to develop a basic approach to how they will identify the risks that exist in their projects and respond to them—a **risk management plan**. The main objectives of this chapter are to help project leaders identify risks within their own projects and sharpen the skills they need to manage those risks.

For our purposes, **risk** is defined as some probability that a problem will emerge in a project and have a negative impact on it.[1] The basic approach we will use for presenting our risk management plan is given in Figure 5.1 and covers three major topics. The first deals with how project leaders can

Figure 5.1   Overview of the Risk Management Process

- Identify a Risk
  - *Sources of risk:* Project management, the host organization, deliverables, the external environment
- Assess the Risk
  - *Risk assessment:* Judge the likelihood and possible impact of potential problems
- Respond to the Risk
  - *Risk responses:* Accept, avoid, reduce, or transfer the risk

ESTABLISHING A RISK RESPONSE PLAN

- Who is involved, what they should be doing, and when

DEALING WITH RISK IN PROJECT EXECUTION

- Monitor and Respond to Risk
  - Review known risk and look for new problems
- Review Risk Performance
  - Develop lessons learned for the rest of the project

---

look for and respond to potential problems in their project planning. As project leaders develop and review their plans, they keep an eye out for potential problems. When they spot one, they assess how much of a threat it is—how likely the problem will occur and, if so, how bad it could be. Finally, they decide how to respond to the problem. With smaller threats, leaders may simply accept them and move on. With larger risks, however, they likely will try to handle them by changing their plans in some way to avoid the problems they find, reduce their likely harm, or transfer the risk they pose to others. This process is repeated over and over as project leaders develop and review their plans. A large part of the chapter is devoted to issues important to this process: where to look for sources of risk, how to assess risk, and how to respond to it.

Risk is never completely removed, of course, so project leaders need to develop a risk response plan to handle risk as the project moves forward—the problems that still remain and the new ones that are sure to emerge. This will be our second topic of discussion. We look at who should be involved and what they should do. Our third topic will be related to how project leaders can monitor and respond to risk during actual project execution.

In this chapter we will give a lot of detailed attention to the conceptual and technical tools of risk management. Good risk management, however, does not lie only in the use of these tools. It depends as well on how everyone in the project approaches the job. It is worthwhile, then, to take a moment, here at the beginning of the chapter, to discuss what it takes for a project to manage risk well. This discussion is relevant to everything else we cover in this chapter.

GOOD RISK MANAGEMENT

Good risk management is not an activity that a project leader does once or twice during a project. It is, rather, a general orientation to the project that is the responsibility of everyone working on it. Good risk management starts in the project initiation process with careful consideration of what the project is supposed to achieve and how it is to be done—whether it is worth doing, whether it is possible to pull off, and, if so, what it will realistically take to do so. As project plans are developed, good risk management asks many questions, but three are repeated over and over: "What is missing?" "What can go wrong?" and "Is this enough?" When projects plans are finished, they are reviewed once more with fresh eyes and more challenging questions. Importantly, good risk management enlists the aid of others in planning and review: specialists in technical areas; key team members with knowledge, skills, and experience; others with experience in similar projects or project components; and those upon whom the project might depend—clients, end users, vendors, subcontractors, and the boss are all invited to the table at one time or another, in one way or another.

Projects develop good risk management when it becomes a project habit. Everyone keeps an eye out for potential and emerging problems and responds to them as early as possible. No one keeps problems secret, because problems are seen as challenges to be resolved together, not blamed on those who find them. Time is set aside at regular meetings to address possible risks and coordinate responses to them. And every once in a while, at important times in the project, people take the time to look back, ask some basic questions, and learn from their answers: What problems did we catch, what did we miss, when did we do well, where could we improve, what changes need to be made? With this in mind, then, we turn our attention to the conceptual and technical tools used in risk management starting with where to look for risk.

SOURCES OF RISK

When project leaders develop and review their project plans, they need to know what kinds of risk to look for. Of course, risk comes from so many sources that it is impossible to identify them all. We can, however, identify some of the more common areas where problems are found. These include problems that often emerge from the management of the project itself, from the host organization, from the risks involved when producing project deliverables, and from a wide range of external sources. [2] As noted above, the right kinds of people can help a great deal in finding potential problems.

RISKS FROM PROJECT MANAGEMENT

Project risks are potential problems with the project itself—its planning and execution. We will look at some of the problems that might come up in project planning, and then turn our attention to project execution.

Project Planning

Project planning is no easy task, and a number of mistakes can be made that will likely produce problems later on. Mistakes are even more likely to be made when there is pressure to get a project started, which is most often the case. Spending a little extra time in planning and review, however, can save a lot of time and money later on. Risks in the planning phase often center on the development of the work breakdown structure (WBS), estimations of costs and time requirements, staffing issues, and logistics.

The WBS is the foundation of any project. Because it defines the work that will be done in the project, it is the basis for estimating virtually all project needs, costs, and time requirements. Anything missed, then, can produce a host of other problems. Unfortunately, as we note in Chapter 3, it is all too easy to overlook important work requirements. In fact, many believe that failing to identify all necessary project work is the number one cause of project problems.

In the development of project plans, then, a challenging job is to find what tasks are *not* included in the WBS that should be. As we noted in Chapter 3, one often overlooked area of project work is that of the necessary support tasks, which help leaders administer and manage the project. In addition to the core tasks that produce deliverables, these support tasks need attention during the planning process as well.

Cost and time estimates for the work to be done present another challenge. Some estimates can be straightforward if the work to be done is fairly simple. More complex work or work new to the project leader, however, requires careful assessment based on expert inputs, standards, and other supporting resources. [3]

Staffing problems can emerge in a number of ways, but most can be summed up in terms of three considerations: whether (a) there is enough staff with

(b) the right capabilities to do the job (c) when you need them. Staffing is one of the more costly project items, and project leaders have a tendency to assume staff can do more than they actually can. This eventually leaves the project with too little staff. The capabilities of staff to successfully complete their work can be another problem. Staff skills, of course, need to be considered, but a broader look at what team members are supposed to do is important as well. Chief Sessions, for example, faces the possible loss of a police chief from his project if the new city manager is unhappy with the project review. That police chief not only has important skills but other resources that are critical to the success of the project (e.g., position authority over his department). This leads us to our third consideration—whether staff with critical capabilities will be around when needed. The chief of police may be pulled out of the project by the new city manager, but critical staff may leave for many other reasons as well. These possible problems can become more troublesome when the host organization is volunteering staff for its own projects.

Logistics—getting the right tools, material, and other resources to the project when they are needed—is another common problem in projects. This problem can cause even more harm when the resources needed are critical to project work and in short supply. In development and review of project plans, then, thinking back through the "supply chain" of resources required for a job is an important area of risk assessment.

Project Execution

Once projects are launched, they still require a great deal of attention from their project leaders. Due consideration, for example, needs to be given to command and control of the project and to project processes like communications.

In terms of command and control, leaders need to pay attention to the leadership structure. In small projects, all team members might report to the project leader. In larger projects, more attention needs to be given to who reports to whom. This makes sure that unity of effort, unity of command, and accountability for getting the project done is well established. Project milestones also need to be scheduled so that project reviews are timely. Tools used to monitor and control the project (e.g., the project schedule and budget tools like earned value analysis—see Appendix B) need to be reviewed and then effectively used. Just as important, project leaders, particularly those new to project management, need to review their own leadership role as well as their knowledge of and commitment to the time demands the project will place on them.

Project and team processes like communications, coordination, decision making, and quality control need attention as well. Are communications getting the right information to the right people when needed? Are different parts of the project coming together when they need to? Are the best people involved in project decisions? Are deliverables meeting performance requirements in a timely fashion? The answers to these questions signal whether the underlying processes are working properly or are producing problems that need attention before they become larger and more costly.

RISKS FROM THE HOST ORGANIZATION

Organizational risks are potential problems the host organization may give the project. That risk increases when the host organization has a reputation for acting in unpredictable ways. There are at least three common sources of organizational risk—the extent of organizational support, project funding, and the possibility of political problems.

Organizational Support

Organizational support is one of the most important organizational considerations. It includes the support of higher management as well as others who have authority and influence over the project. Their level of support is the extent to which the project is a priority for them and for the organization. From the first moment of project inception to project close down, the support of higher management and influential organizational stakeholders will play a large role in project success. Certainly, planning for and maintaining such support must be given due consideration.

Funding and Other Resource Support

Projects require funding and resource support to accomplish their goals. Even when outside clients are the source of project funds, the host organization can present problems. What comes in from clients rarely goes entirely to the project, and internal rules and procedures of the host organization can hamper funding flow as well. Multiyear projects present their own funding risks because reviews, contingences, and changing priorities produce uncertainty.

Organizations that host their own projects often provide projects with a mix of funds and "volunteered" organizational resources from other departments. In addition to the reliability of funding, possible resistance from these other sources of support needs to be considered and addressed. These kinds of problems are even more troublesome in situations like those faced by Chief Sessions—when the host organization is actually a partnership of multiple organizations.

Organizational Politics

Unfortunately, organizational politics can also be a real source of project risk for a number of reasons. In project organizations, for example, there is often competition—sometimes fierce—over project resources and priorities. When projects are aimed at instituting some kind of organizational change, vested interests can line up for and against that change. Finally, project leaders who successfully finish their projects can receive recognition and rewards that others may desire. All of these situations can lead to political problems. When organizational politics emerge, political players tend to use whatever power and authority they may have to achieve their ends. This almost always produces problems for a project. Therefore, it is important to consider who will be affected by the conduct and outcomes of a project—and whether they will be allies or foes.

DELIVERABLE RISKS

Projects are planned and executed to produce one or more deliverables. Those deliverables, in turn, comply with specifications and, perhaps, must perform in some way to achieve the objectives of the project. **Deliverable risks** are the risks that project deliverables will not meet intended quality or performance requirements. The technical risk associated with producing new products is the most often discussed type of deliverable risk. More common problems, however, come from other sources, especially in smaller projects.

Technical Problems

Some projects must produce products that push the boundaries of what is technically possible. The development of a new aircraft, for example, may require the development of new composites for the construction of its wings or engines. Pharmaceutical firms face similar challenges in developing new compounds for the treatment of some disease. Because the technology does not yet exist to produce such deliverables, there is inherent risk to the project, and it can often be quite high.

Other Problems

Deliverable risk, however, is not restricted to projects that are pushing the boundaries of science and technology. Consider, for example, a project to implement a total quality change in production methods. The changes required in procedures, machinery, and personnel can challenge a project team in the same way engineers can be challenged by developing new technology.

At least two issues need to be considered when addressing deliverable risk, whether that risk comes from high-tech or more conventional projects. The first issue is how easy it will be to achieve product or service outcomes. Some deliverables are easy to produce, and others may be quite difficult for the project team. As difficulties rise, more costs and project time may be required. The second issue is related to how demanding clients are about the exact characteristics of project deliverables. The more exacting clients are, the more care, cost, and time must be given to a project.[4]

EXTERNAL RISKS

External risks are the problems that might come from the larger project environment. We start by looking at problems clients and end users might give the project. We then consider risk posed by resource suppliers, followed by regulations, the broader commercial market, and, finally, the physical environment.

Clients and End Users

As principal stakeholders, clients often cause problems for the project once it has begun by changing the specifications or performance requirements of deliverables, adjusting funding, or asking for additional products and services (scope creep). The new city manager in the Crime Tracking Project is one example of this very common problem. Her review will likely result in a number of changes she will want the project to make.

End users, those who will ultimately use some or all of the deliverables produced, can also be a source of problems even though they are not the actual client. For example, the patrol officers in the opening case are end users who may require more training and upgrades to the on-board computers they use.

Vendors and Other Suppliers

Projects often depend on vendors and other resource suppliers, such as subcontractors, to deliver quality products and services to support project work (e.g., office supplies, communications equipment, transportation, tools, raw materials, etc.). In addition, vendors and others often produce actual project deliverables as well (e.g., the on-board computers and training produced by Patrol Computers). The quality of these resources and timeliness of their delivery are risks to consider. Risk to the project increases as it depends more on specific suppliers and specific, hard-to-replace resources.

Regulatory Problems

Projects often require some sort of regulatory approval, and project leaders must pay close attention to the regulatory requirements in their projects. Regulators and the regulations they enforce can literally shut down a project—as happened with Chief Sessions—or render its deliverables useless (e.g., failed building inspections). Projects need to be examined very closely for points where approvals are required. Ensuring that the project or its deliverables achieve approval will likely require a fair amount of project work, cost, and time.[5]

Market Dynamics

A story is often told in marketing classes about a large consumer products firm that routinely interfered with the test marketing of products from competing organizations. When the competing organizations test marketed their products, this firm would aggressively discount its own competing products and offer free giveaways to affect the results of the test marketing.

Most projects will not have to worry about this kind of direct interference. Competitors often have plans and products of their own, however, that can interfere with the marketability of a project's deliverables or with the conduct of the project itself. Consumer electronics firms, for example, face fierce competition from the design and performance of competing products (e.g., computers, cell phones, digital cameras, and the like). This market reality, in turn, places extreme time demands on product development. It also adds a great deal of risk in terms of whether the new products will match or exceed the performance of competing products.

Market forces also produce risk for the delivery of project resources. Builders, for example, can face unexpected problems from the demands of other builders for needed products, labor, and services. As another example, supply chains are often overtaxed by competing companies working to get their products on store shelves for the Christmas buying season.

The Physical Environment

Weather conditions, of course, can have a direct impact on any project that requires outside work. But weather conditions can have an indirect impact on projects as well. Hurricanes in the Gulf of Mexico, for example, can affect the costs of building materials by causing extensive damage to Gulf Coast communities. Even if you are a developer in Virginia, hurricane season can affect your costs and is a source of risk.

Weather is not the only element of the physical environment that can affect the conduct or outcomes of projects. Temperatures and noise levels within buildings can affect projects as well. For example, training sessions can be affected by noise levels, lighting, and temperature in the building. A moment to consider how the physical environment might affect the conduct of work in a project or the delivery of its products and services, then, is well worth the time.

LOOKING FOR RISK

We have spent a number of pages listing potential problems that might come up in a project, but we have only scratched the surface. Although the problems we looked at are very common ones, project leaders should consider inviting knowledgeable others to review project plans and help spot potential problems. Technical experts, knowledgeable project personnel, and those with experience in similar projects are some people leaders may ask for assistance.

As we mentioned above, the process of risk identification and response is usually repeated throughout the project: A problem is spotted, its risk is assessed, and some response is made before moving on to the next problem. We turn now to the second step in that process—how a potential problem is assessed—before deciding on some course of action to deal with it.

RISK ASSESSMENT

Recall that risk is the probability that some problem will have a negative impact on the project in the future. **Risk assessment**, then, has two parts: assessing the probability that the problem will occur and assessing the potential harm it might produce. Most often, qualitative judgments are made about project risks, but sometimes more sophisticated quantitative assessments are made as well.

QUALITATIVE ASSESSMENTS OF RISK

Qualitative assessments of risk are broad judgments about whether a particular problem will emerge in the project and, if so, what kind of impact it is likely to have. These judgments are often based on the knowledge and experience of project leaders and those helping them to make those judgments.

The mathematical probability that a problem will arise during a project technically ranges from 0% to 100%. Qualitative judgments, however, more often use a 3-point scale (i.e., *low, medium*, and *high*) or a 5-point scale (i.e., from *very low* to *very high*) to measure likelihood of occurrence.

Judgments about how much *harm* a problem may produce will use a similar ranking. Just what *kind* of an impact a problem might have, however, is an important issue in making those judgments. At least three kinds of negative impact should be considered: budgetary, time, and quality impacts. **Budgetary impact** is how much the problem will increase the costs of the project or reduce its funding. **Time impact** is how much the problem will increase the time it will take to get the project done. **Quality impact** is how much the problem will hurt the quality or performance of deliverables. Project leaders should also feel free to add project impacts important to them. One such impact could be "headaches"—how much hassle something might cause![6]

The qualitative approach is enough for most projects to assess the risk of potential problems. This is because the primary purpose of a risk assessment is to decide whether to take the next step—to develop some sort of response to the problem. The qualitative approach is often good enough to determine which potential problems need to be addressed.

QUANTITATIVE ASSESSMENTS OF RISK

Quantitative assessments take qualitative assessments a few steps further. They use more sophisticated tools, techniques, and methods to estimate the mathematical probabilities that problems might occur and specific assessments of their impact (e.g., in terms of dollar costs or actual measures of time). The advantage of quantitative assessments is that they can be used in a variety of numerical analyses. For example, the probability that a problem will occur (e.g., 50%) and its cost if it does (e.g., $5,000.00) can be multiplied together to establish the **expected value of a problem** (e.g., $2,500.00). These expected values can be used, in turn, to rank project risks in terms of potential cost. They can also be used to evaluate possible courses of action. If a proposed action will cost more than the cost of the problem itself, for example, the action is not **cost-effective** and should be set aside.

Another use of quantitative assessments was mentioned in Chapter 4 when discussing how Monte Carlo routines can be used to assess time risks to the project schedule. Recall that Program Evaluation and Review Technique (PERT) schedules provide optimistic, likely, and pessimistic estimates of the time it will take to complete each task. Monte Carlo techniques can take those individual estimates and assess their combined impact on the project as a whole or on any individual part of it.

After finding a potential problem and assessing its likely harm, the next step is to decide what should be done about the problem. As we will see, most problems judged to pose little or no real threat will simply be accepted. Other, larger problems, however, will require more thought about how to handle them. This is the issue to which we turn now—how to respond to the risk posed by a problem.

RISK RESPONSES

There are at least four ways risk can be handled by project leaders. They can simply accept the risk, try to avoid it completely, try to reduce the risk, or transfer the risk somewhere else.[7]

ACCEPT THE RISK

Accepting risk means that, although the risk remains known, nothing is done about it. Most problems that have a low probability of happening or a low level of negative impact are often simply accepted in the development and review of project plans. Nothing is done about these risks. Problems that are slightly more worrisome but still accepted may receive a more proactive strategy—contingency planning. A **contingency plan** is a plan to do something about a problem if and when it does come up. Contingency plans often have **triggers**—a set of conditions that indicate the problem is beginning to emerge. At that point, the contingency plans are reviewed and put into action to address the problem. For example, Chief Sessions might have made it a point to keep an eye out for potential problems with funding (e.g., online reports of federal cutbacks to the government program funding projects like his). At that point, he could start modifying his project budget with cost cutting in some areas to support other, higher priority work.

AVOID THE RISK

Avoiding risk generally involves changing or eliminating the conditions that will lead to the problem. One common example of this is when work is found to be missing from a WBS. That work is immediately added to the

WBS to avoid the problems of not including it. In the Crime Tracking Project, Chief Sessions could have avoided the problem with Patrol Computers if he had known that they really don't deliver and support quality products. Then, he could have chosen another vendor from the very start.

Additionally, the risk associated with particularly demanding or risky project deliverables might be avoided by dropping them from the project altogether or by dropping some of their performance requirements. For example, Chief Sessions may have found that other communities were able to deliver a wide range of services using the same data-sharing system he proposed. Some of those services, however, would be far easier to deliver than others. When first developing the project charter, then, Chief Sessions could have focused on including the easier deliverables and avoided the more difficult ones. Those more difficult deliverables could be either left to the future or added as a "bonus" if they can be delivered within cost and time constraints.

REDUCE THE RISK

Reducing risk involves decreasing the probability of a problem occurring and/or the level of its harm. More careful selection of project staff or additional training, for example, can reduce the likelihood of errors due to lack of knowledge and experience. Careful testing and inspection procedures can reduce the probability of poor products or services being delivered to the client. Another example can be found in the Crime Tracking Project. Chief Sessions knew that one of the city managers was about to retire. That city manager and the chief could have worked with the City Council to stress the importance of the project when hiring the new city manager. In addition, the chief could have arranged to meet with the new city manager early on—with influential City Council members who liked the project—to pave the way for its acceptance. Another option would have been a contract between all the cities to ensure their commitment to the project and its objectives.

TRANSFER THE RISK

Transferring risk involves transferring the risk to some other person or organization. Some cost risks can be transferred by covering the risk with insurance. Movie production companies, for example, often insure top actors in their production projects so that if something were to happen to them, any losses would be covered. Risks of dealing with vendors could be transferred to the vendors themselves by contracting for warranties on the products and services they provide. For example, "performance clauses" might have been added to the contract Chief Sessions made with Patrol Computers. If the training or computers did not perform according to specifications, the company would have to fix the computers and cover related project costs. Arrangements like insurance and warrantees, however, often add additional project costs that need to be judged in terms of their cost-effectiveness.

Sometimes risks can be transferred by "outsourcing" them. For example, a particular deliverable might have high quality risk because project staff do not have the time or ability to produce it according to client specifications. In this kind of situation, a subcontract might be developed with an outside organization to develop the product or service. Of course, the project is responsible for the deliverable even if it is produced by a subcontractor.

Cost risks might even be transferred to the client. One way this is done is by negotiating "cost-plus" terms where the client covers the eventual cost of one or more deliverables plus a certain percentage or amount for profit. Another way this is done is to negotiate risk contingencies. If certain problems do emerge, the client agrees to cover additional specified costs, grant the project more time to deal with the problem, or make some other arrangements.

Project leaders should remember that although the risk of potential problems can be transferred to others, the actual impact of those problems on the project may still hurt relations with important stakeholders. Problems that impact the cost, time, or deliverables of a project will almost always have a negative impact on the expectations of stakeholders. It is important, then, to work closely with those stakeholders to manage those expectations from project initiation to closing. We will look more closely at this issue in Chapter 7.

To this point, we have discussed some of the problems that can come up in a project and how to assess their likelihood and potential impact. We also have discussed some of the options project leaders have for dealing with those risks. Following these steps does not mean, however, that a project will be free from risk. Next, we address the need for a plan to monitor and respond to additional risks that can affect the project during execution.

ESTABLISHING A RISK RESPONSE PLAN

Even when an excellent job has been done to identify, assess, and respond to project risk, there will always remain **residual risk**—the risk that remains after risk responses have been developed. Some risks will have escaped detection. Also, adjustments made to address the primary risks found will carry secondary risks of their own—risks caused by addressing those primary risks. Changing one vendor for another, for example, reduces the risk associated with the first vendor but adds risk from the second. As project leaders move into project execution, they need to keep an eye out not only for the risks that have been identified but for new problems that will surely emerge. That is the purpose of a **risk response plan**—a plan that assigns project personnel to monitor identified problems, keep a lookout for new ones, and develop action plans for doing so.

One important part of a risk response plan is a list that keeps track of potential problems—a **risk register**. Those problems are described along with where they are likely to emerge in the project. Triggers might also be described—those conditions that signal that a problem is beginning to emerge. Finally, "risk owners" are assigned to keep an eye out for potential problems. **Risk owners** are project staff who are responsible for monitoring and responding to risks—usually those risks associated with their parts of the project.

Another important part of the risk response plan is an action plan for monitoring and responding to project risk. We will cover this more fully below, but at the very least, this would include periodic reviews of risk as the project moves forward.

The risk processes described can seem very complex, time-consuming, and involved. Sometimes they are. In very large government projects, for example, unforeseen problems can cost millions of dollars. So risk identification, assessment, and response can be quite complex and costly as well. In smaller projects, risk assessment is more straightforward. Working with others, project leaders take care in the development and review of their plans to focus on problems that might come up in a project.

Although looking for and responding to risk can add time and cost to project planning, the benefits usually far outweigh the cost. There are at least three important benefits of looking for, assessing, and responding to risk in the development and review of project plans. The first is that the project plan gets better as needed changes are made to the WBS, the schedule, the budget, staffing, and the like when thinking through project risk. The second is that project risk is reduced as plans are modified to take care of them. And the third benefit is that project leaders become more knowledgeable about the project and the contingencies they are to face.

DEALING WITH RISK IN PROJECT EXECUTION

As the project moves into the execution stage, the risk response plan is put into action by monitoring and responding to risk when it emerges. Also, project leaders and others can get better at identifying and responding to problems if they take the time for periodic reviews to assess how well they have done. These reviews can produce "lessons learned" for the project yet to be done and for projects in the future.

MONITOR AND RESPOND TO RISK

Time should be set aside at regular project meetings to address project risk. In addition to the potential problems that have been identified in the risk response plan, risk owners need to discuss new, emerging problems in their part of the project—particularly with those who might be affected by them. Plans to deal with the problem should generally be shared as well. This is important not only because other team members need to be informed, but also because they may be able to improve response plans or identify secondary risks that the risk owner had not considered. If other project staff need to be involved in the problem or its response, these meetings also help to coordinate their roles. Usually the results of the response will be included as an agenda item in a subsequent meeting.

This is not to say, of course, that every potential and emerging problem needs to be formally addressed by the project team. Risk owners should have the knowledge, skills, and authority to handle problems within their skill set. If those problems can produce real harm to the project, however, or if they affect the operations of others in the team, they should be shared with the team for a coordinated response.

Before leaving this topic a few things need to be said about the manner in which project leaders handle risk and project problems. How they do so will have a large impact on how risk identification and management will actually be handled by their staff. Few project leaders like dealing with project problems, and who can blame them? Problems often mean more costs, slipped schedules, risk to deliverables, and lots of headaches and stress as responses are developed and implemented.

However, project leaders need to *welcome* the discovery of problems by project staff. Project personnel are all too aware of what can happen to the "bearer of bad news." When that bad news reflects problems within their own operations, project staff will be particularly reluctant to report them. This may result in problems being ignored until they have grown so large that they can no longer be hidden or dealt with easily.

Although it may not be human nature to do so, project leaders need to welcome receiving such bad news if they wish the project team to give honest, frank, and timely evaluations of emerging problems. Welcoming project problems doesn't mean celebrating them, but it does mean holding back criticism and focusing on the problem itself and its response, not blame. Hopefully, project leaders can also bring risk owners into the resolution of the problem. Doing so can help risk owners develop their own knowledge and skills in problem identification and response. With the help of the risk owners, the project leader might also learn if there are broader reasons for not only that problem, but those that may be similar to it.

REVIEW RISK PERFORMANCE

Finally, as the project moves forward, project leaders can also benefit from looking backward. As important milestones are reached, leaders should review problems that have emerged and how they were dealt with. These reviews can inform leaders and others on the team not only about new problems that might be emerging, but about how well project staff responded to the problems they have encountered. The lessons learned, then, can be applied to the rest of project as it moves forward.

Table 5.1   Risk Management Check-Off List

Listed here are a few important questions project leaders may wish to ask themselves as they assess the risks of their project and plan how to respond to them. The questions are meant to be used as a point of departure, to help encourage project leaders to think through the issues involved in managing project risk. Leaders should add other questions as they see fit.

Sources of Risk

- Risks From the Project Itself
  - Have I consulted with others who are more familiar with the kinds of work in the project than I am?
  - Have all the core tasks needed to produce the deliverables been included in the WBS? Have all support tasks needed to administer and manage the project been included?
  - Have cost and time estimates been reviewed? Are the foundations of those estimates sound?
  - Do I have enough staff to complete the project? Do they have the right skills, and will they be available when I need them?

(Continued)

Table 5.1 (Continued)

- o Have all the tools, materials, and other resources needed for the project been considered and integrated into the plan? Will they be delivered to the project when they are needed?
- o *Communications:* Is the right information reaching those who need it when they need it?
- o *Decision making:* Are the right people involved in decision making? Are decisions causing additional problems? Are decisions being made in a timely manner?
- o *Quality control:* Are support and core tasks meeting expected levels of quality?
- o *Coordination:* Is there unity of effort and unity of command in the project? Is project work coming together as planned?
- o *Command and control:* Is the project producing its deliverables according to budget and according to schedule?

- Risks From the Host Organization
  - o Does the project have the support of key members of higher management? Is the project a high-priority one? What do I need to do to ensure that support as the project moves forward?
  - o Is there enough funding to complete the project? Will those funds be available when they are needed?
  - o If resources have been committed from the host organization, have the sources of that support been consulted to determine their level of commitment? What do I need to do to ensure those commitments as the project moves forward?
  - o Who in the host organization might be helped or harmed by the conduct of the project or its planned outcomes? How much resistance or interference can I expect? Whom might I go to for support other than higher management?

- Deliverable Risks
  - o Are there any unusual technical challenges to producing the project's deliverables? If so, do I have the personnel required to meet those challenges? Does the work scope include any testing that might need to be done? Is the client aware of the challenges and needs of these deliverables?
  - o What are the specifications or performance requirements of my deliverables? How exacting are those requirements?
  - o How much tolerance does the client have for variation in deliverables?
  - o Is the client aware of those problems that might arise and what might be needed to address them?

- External Risks
  - Does the client fully understand and agree to the costs, time, and deliverables of the project? How understanding is the client in terms of project problems that may affect the deliverables? Have the end users of the deliverables been fully considered and their needs integrated into the specifications and performance requirements of the deliverables?
  - Are the resource suppliers to the project dependable in terms of delivery and resource quality? Does anything need to be done to ensure these?
  - What, if any, regulations apply to the conduct or output of the project? Who is responsible for conducting regulatory reviews? What is expected? What is needed to ensure passage of regulatory reviews?
  - Does my project work need to consider market competitors? If so, how might they affect the project or its output?
  - Are there any external environmental conditions (e.g., the weather) or internal environmental conditions (e.g., sound levels, temperatures) that could affect the running of the project or its deliverables?

- Do I Have a Plan to Look for and Respond to Risk During the Project?
  - Who will look out for problems? Consider assigning that responsibility to those who are working on the parts of the project where problems may emerge.
  - Do they know what to look out for and how they may respond?

Questions to Ask During the Execution of the Project

- Monitoring and Review of Problems by Risk Owners
  - Are problems being spotted early and being dealt with effectively?
  - Are potential risks and problems being shared with others in the project when they affect them?

- Project Reviews
  - Are periodic reviews being made about how well the project is proceeding? Are the lessons learned being implemented as needed in the project?

SUMMARY

All projects carry risk—some likelihood that problems will emerge in the project to negatively affect it. To deal with this risk, project managers need a risk management plan—an approach to identify possible problems, assess them, and respond to them in the planning and execution of the project.

Risk comes from many sources, and project leaders can benefit from the help of others in uncovering potential problems. Some possible advisors in this process include technical experts, important team members, other stakeholders, as well as those who have experience with similar projects. Problems can emerge from within the management of the project itself, from the host organization, from the actual production of deliverables, and from the larger project environment.

Risks from project management often come from problems with project planning. Many of these risks can be addressed by checking the work breakdown structure (WBS) to make sure all needed work is accounted for. Leaders should also check cost and time estimates to make sure they are reasonable. Leaders should review project staffing carefully, as well, to make sure there are enough staff members with the right capabilities available to the project when they are needed. Finally, a review of project logistics makes sure that the right tools, materials, and other resources will come to the project when they are needed. Beyond planning, project execution needs attention as well. In terms of command and control, the leadership structure in the project needs to work in a coordinated way so that unity of command and effort is achieved. The leadership should work together to establish milestones and complete timely project reviews. Project management tools like the project schedule and the project budget need to be used on an ongoing basis to catch problems as they come up. And leaders need to make sure project processes are working as they should. Communications, coordination, decision making, and quality control are all processes that need careful attention.

The host organization can also present the project with potential problems. Project leaders need to make sure their project is a priority for the organization and that they are getting the support they need from higher management. Funding and resource flow from or through the organization needs careful attention to make sure funds and resources arrive when needed. Unfortunately, organizational politics can be another source of risk, and project leaders need to assess how others are affected by the project and whether they support it.

Deliverable risk is still another area of potential problems. Often, technical problems can emerge in production of deliverables. The more deliverables push at the edge of available technology, the more problems can emerge in their development. But deliverable risk comes from sources other than these high technical demands. Anything that can get in the way of deliverables being produced or working properly needs to get the full attention of project leaders. Deliverable risk increases as deliverables become more complex and as clients become more demanding. And as deliverable risk increases, more care, cost, and time will need to be devoted to addressing it.

External risks from the broader project environment need attention as well. Common problems can come from clients and end users as well as resource suppliers. Clients and end users may wish to change the specifications or performance requirements of deliverables, for example, or add new deliverables to the project. Vendors and other resource suppliers become more of a risk the more the project depends on them for the quality and timely delivery of their resources.

External project risk also comes from having to meet regulations, dealing with the broader market, and even the physical environment of the project. Whatever regulations will apply to the project need to be considered carefully. Project leaders should make sure that the appropriate time and effort is devoted to addressing them, or the project could be delayed or even shut down. The broader market can be a source of problems for some projects as well. Sometimes, for example, competitors can create problems for the marketability of a project's deliverables or for the availability of resources both they and the project need. Finally, even the physical environment needs to be considered. When projects require outside work, the weather needs to be considered. The weather can also impact a project if it impacts the delivery of its resources. Even the environment indoors (e.g., noise levels and internal temperatures) can affect the running of some projects or the delivery of their products and services.

Once potential problems are found in a project, they need to be assessed in terms of how likely they are to occur and how big of a problem they are likely to be. This kind of risk assessment usually makes use of informed judgment in qualitative assessments of risk. Judgments about the probability and impact of a problem often range between low, medium, and high. Quantitative assessments of risk use more precise quantitative measures. Potential problems that are more likely to occur and have a higher negative impact get more attention in terms of how to respond to them.

There are four basic methods of responding to risk: accept the risk, avoid it, reduce it, or transfer the risk to another person or organization. Smaller problems are often simply accepted. Larger problems might also be accepted, but contingency plans are often made in case they actually do occur—triggered by some signal that they are emerging. Some problems can be avoided if the conditions that lead to them can be changed or avoided. Another resource supplier might be chosen, for example, if one is judged as too risky.

Risk can be reduced if the probability of a problem occurring or its potential harm can be reduced. Careful selection of good personnel, for example, can reduce the probability that they will make mistakes in the project. Finally, risk can be transferred to others. Projects sometimes take out insurance on important assets, for example, or require performance contracts with their resource providers.

There will always be some residual risk left in any project despite the best efforts of project leaders. Even good responses made to likely problems can produce secondary risks of their own. It is important, then, to have a risk response plan for the project. That plan will identify the risk owners—those who will be watching for risks already identified as well as any new risks that may emerge in their part of the project. It is a good practice to keep a description of identified risks and when they might come up in a project in a "risk register." How potential problems will be monitored and what responses will be made are other components of the risk response plan.

Once a project gets under way, risk owners should address emerging problems at regular staff meetings. This allows others to be aware of these problems, assess their impact on their own part of the project, and, perhaps, offer suggestions on how to respond to them. Hopefully, most new problems can be handled by their risk owners. Those that cannot or those that impact other parts of the project should definitely be brought to the attention of the project team and its leaders. When problems are brought to project leaders, they need to focus on their solution, not on blaming or punishing those who revealed the problem. Otherwise, project personnel will be reluctant to bring them up until they are too large to ignore and, usually, tougher and more costly to address. Finally, periodic reviews should be made of how well the project has handled problems. Lessons learned from such reviews can help leaders and others handle problems better in the future.

REVIEW QUESTIONS

1. Define risk, and explain the basic structure of the risk management process.

2. What does it take to accomplish good risk management practices?

3. Risk can originate from a number of sources within and around the project.
   a. List and describe the four most common areas of the project where risks can originate.
   b. List and discuss at least two types of risk for each area.

4. Risk assessment has two parts. Discuss and describe those two parts and how they relate to each other.

5. What are the four ways that a project team can respond to a risk? Describe and provide an example of each.

6. What is the purpose of a risk response plan? What is a risk owner, and who should be appointed to own risk? What is a risk owner's role in the risk response plan?

7. How should project leaders address risk during the execution phase of a project?

EXERCISES

1. Think back to a project you have worked on in the past.

   a. Were there any risks that the team noticed and responded to before they became problems? If so, what was the source of those problems? How did the team handle those risks? Why did the team decide to handle them in that way?

   b. What were the major problems that did interfere with the project? What was the source of those problems?

   c. If you were to go back now, how would you respond to those problems before they came up?

   d. Did the team come up with a risk response plan? If so, describe it. If not, what suggestions would you make now to your past self regarding a risk response plan?

2. Briefly describe a project in which you are currently involved.

   a. List at least three possible risks to the project and identify their source.

   b. Assess the amount of impact they will have on the project, using both qualitative and quantitative means. For the quantitative assessment, use real data if possible. If not, feel free to estimate values.

   c. Finally, suggest ways your team could address those risks, and draft a risk response plan for doing so.

ENDNOTES

1. The Project Management Body of Knowledge (PMBOK) 2008 defines risk as including possible beneficial outcomes for the project. These are ignored here, but project leaders might well want to be on the outlook for "positive risk" as well. See The Project Management Institute. (2008). *A guide to the project management body of knowledge*. Newtown Square, PA: Author.

2. Many of the sources of risk come from stakeholders in the project. We give them closer attention when focusing on the environment that surrounds the project in Chapter 7. These risk categories are from the PMBOK 2008.

3. Host organizations often "volunteer" human and other resources from the organization for project work. Often, time and costs are overlooked or minimized in these cases, and it is a mistake to do so. At the very least, careful time estimates should be made for those resources others depend on (e.g., personnel from other departments). Cost estimates of personnel can also be made using their salary data and project time needs. These represent the "opportunity costs" of volunteered personnel.

4. This kind of sensitivity is part of a larger idea of "risk sensitivity"—how sensitive a principal stakeholder is to variations in costs, time, and deliverables.

5. In some projects, the regulatory process can take months, even years, to work through with uncertain outcomes. Projects facing such daunting risk are often not approved because of it. Even seemingly small approvals like building and fire inspections can cause countless problems for a project. I recently worked with an international firm that had a project of rolling out hundreds of new, company-owned retail outlets across the United States in the span of a single year. One of the most troublesome problems they faced was from approvals required by fire marshals and building inspectors.

6. Some personnel, for example, might be more trouble than they are worth. The PMBOK 2008 provides other criteria to consider in addition to these.

7. These risk response categories are taken and adapted from the PMBOK 2008.

KEY TERMS

Accepting Risk: when nothing is done about a problem, even though the risk is known.

Avoiding Risk: when the conditions that will lead to a problem are changed or eliminated.

Budgetary Impact: how much the problem will increase the costs of the project or reduce its funding.

Contingency Plan: a plan to do something about a problem if and when it does come up.

Cost-Effective Risk Solutions: when a proposed action to deal with a problem will cost less than the likely cost of the problem itself.

Deliverable Risks: the risks that project deliverables will not meet intended quality or performance requirements.

Expected Value of a Problem: the probability that a problem will occur multiplied by its cost.

External Risks: the problems that might come from the larger project environment—e.g., from clients, end users, suppliers, regulations, the broader commercial market, and the physical environment.

Logistics: getting the right tools, material, and other resources to the project when they are needed.

Organizational Risks: potential problems the host organization may give the project.

Organizational Support: the support of higher management in the host organization as well as others who have authority and influence over the project.

Project Risks: potential problems from within the project itself—its planning and execution.

Qualitative Assessments: broad judgments about whether a particular problem will emerge in the project and, if so, what kind of impact it is likely to have.

Quality Impact: how much the problem will hurt the quality or performance of project deliverables.

Quantitative Assessments: the mathematical probabilities that problems might occur and specific quantitative assessments of their impact.

Reducing Risk: when the probability of a problem occurring and/or the level of its harm is decreased in some way.

Residual Risk: the risk that remains after risk responses have been developed.

Risk: some probability that a problem will emerge in a project and will have a negative impact on it.

Risk Assessment: assessing the probability that problems will occur and assessing the potential harm they may produce.

Risk Management Plan: a basic approach to how project leaders will identify the risks that exist in their projects and how they will respond to them.

Risk Owners: members of the project team who are responsible for monitoring and responding to risks—usually those risks associated with their parts of the project.

Risk Register: a list that keeps track of potential problems.

Risk Response Plan: a plan that assigns project personnel to monitor identified problems, keep a lookout for new ones, and develop action plans for doing so.

Secondary Risks: risks caused by addressing primary risks.

Time Impact: how much the problem will increase the time it will take to get the project done.

Transferring Risk: when the effects of a problem are shifted to some other person or organization.

Triggers: a set of conditions that indicate a specific, known problem is beginning to emerge.

6

Developing Project Teams

INTRODUCTION

THE ACHIEVEMENT PROJECT

Leanne Phillips was more than a little concerned. She had just been put in charge of a tough and politically sensitive project for the Los Padres School District. Recent changes in federal regulations for school districts nationwide required that students demonstrate certain levels of achievement across a number of academic areas for the schools to receive continued funding. Like many school districts across the country, Los Padres had a good record of achievement, but it was still a bit spotty. Some students, particularly those from poorer areas of the district, had continuing difficulty in reaching the achievement levels mandated. This would mean loss in funding if it continued and, in particularly difficult schools, even more drastic action.

Leanne had worked for the district for a number of years and had tracked these changes in federal regulations since they were first developed. The board of supervisors had now called on her to lead a project to address the problem. They wanted her to identify the most critical issues involved in the problem, develop the information they would need to understand and address those issues, and make recommendations about courses of action the board should take. Leanne had an excellent reputation with the board, and she intended to use it to get the resources and help she needed. Along these lines, she realized that she would need an exceptional project team to pull this project off well. The problem of just how to put together such a team began to nag at her.

CHAPTER OVERVIEW

Like many people, Leanne has worked in countless teams. Some of them worked well, but most really did not live up to what she considered true team commitment and success. It seemed that the usual way teams were created was to assemble a bunch of people, say they were now a team, and that was that. She realized that for this particular team to truly be successful, she needed to do far more than that. She had trouble, however, identifying the most important considerations when trying to assemble and develop a successful team.

Unfortunately, there is no prescription for constructing perfect teams. There are, however, a set of key success factors project leaders like Leanne should consider in developing them. This chapter is devoted to reviewing and discussing some of the most important ones. We begin by addressing just what a team *is*. There is a lot of disagreement over the term, and we need to anchor our discussion of what is really meant by the idea of a team. We then move on to consider what counts for team success. If leaders want successful teams, they need to know what counts as success. Next, we examine some of the more critical factors that underpin successful teams. Armed with such knowledge, project leaders can avoid some of the more common problems associated with poorly performing teams. Finally, we examine how teams develop from just a collection of people into a fully functioning team and what they need from project leaders to do so.

WHAT IS A TEAM?

There is a lot of disagreement about just what constitutes a team. The term has been used to refer to any number of groups—from small work groups to entire organizations. In this chapter, we have in mind a specific type of workgroup best defined by Katzenbach and Smith in a *Harvard Business Review* article.[1] They described a **team** as a small number of people with complementary skills who are committed to a common purpose, a common set of performance goals, and a common approach for which they hold themselves mutually accountable.

Katzenbach and Smith highlight a number of important team characteristics, which we will point out now but explore later in more depth. The first characteristic is that teams are usually made up of a small number of team members. As teams become large, they tend to stop acting like a team. A second characteristic is that team members do different kinds of tasks requiring different kinds of knowledge and skills. So-called "**synergy**"—that a team produces more than the simple sum of its individual member contributions—comes from different team members doing different tasks in a coordinated way. To achieve that coordination, different team members must assume work roles that fit together so that the work of one team member fits well with the work of others. A third characteristic is one of direction: Teams have a common purpose and a common set of performance goals. Teams know where they are headed and what must be produced. Fourth, teams have a common "game plan" for how they will achieve their goals. Finally, team activities and performance are controlled. The control of true teams comes from within them—team members hold one another mutually accountable. They review their progress, assess their performance, maintain or alter their plans, and reward and discipline their members to achieve their common goals.

Our focus will be on this kind of team. Even with such a focus, however, looking at project teams is something of a challenge. By far, most of the work done on teams has been oriented to ongoing workgroups—not the kind of temporary teams found in project environments. What we know about the structure, composition, and dynamics of teams, then, will need to be examined with an eye toward the realities and needs of temporary project teams.

WHAT IS A SUCCESSFUL TEAM?

Research on team effectiveness has used a number of criteria for team success.[2] Three of the most important are considered here. They include success in producing client deliverables, promoting team development, and developing team commitment.

SUCCESSFUL TEAMS DELIVER THE GOODS

For a project team to be a success, it must, first and foremost, "deliver the goods." In project teams, that means producing the project's deliverables according to specification, on time, and on budget. That said, in project work, determining what goods need to be delivered—and what their specifications should be—often requires a great deal of leader attention.

Clarifying a project's mission, objectives, and deliverables is a critical early task for any project leader, and we devoted considerable time to it in Chapter 2. Like many other project leaders, Leanne is likely to find this a particularly challenging task. Initially, she will work with her principal client—the board of supervisors—to clarify project objectives and deliverables.

Leanne will soon find, however, that other stakeholders will develop expectations about what the project should produce and how it should be conducted. These other stakeholders will also have some say in determining the extent to which the project is considered a success. Leanne will need the board to champion and support her project. But that likely will not be enough. She will also have to manage the expectations of the other critical stakeholders—a topic we address at length in Chapter 7.

SUCCESSFUL TEAMS GET BETTER

A successful project team is also one that gets better over time. One of the nice things about human capital—unlike most any other kind of capital—is that it can get *better* with use and *increase* rather than diminish in value. Teams should get better, in at least two ways. First, team members should get better in terms of their knowledge, skills, and abilities to produce project deliverables. Second, they should get better at working as a team. Team skills are often overlooked, yet they are essential to successful teams. A simple, conscious attention to developing both task and team skills will go a long way toward team development.

Because project teams are generally thought of as temporary, some leaders may underestimate the value of developing team skills. Many project teams, however, are not so temporary at all. Some teams remain together for years across the life of a large project. Other project teams remain together across a number of different projects (e.g., audit or consulting teams). Still other project teams evolve into permanent work teams once their project is done (e.g., teams brought together to effect some organizational change of which they will be a part). Attention to team development in all these cases will prove to be a wise investment.

Even with truly temporary project teams, however, there is reason to attend to team development. Project leaders often find that they deal with many of the same personnel over a number of projects. Attending to their development not only helps the larger organization but is a good investment in the leader's own future projects. Team members also tend to be more satisfied and committed to project leaders who demonstrate commitment to their development.[3] Finally, attention to team development will pay off in the shorter as well as longer term. Team members can climb project learning curves faster when project leaders help in their development and turn their increased satisfaction and commitment to project needs.

These efforts toward team development can take many forms, but one is particularly appropriate for project work. Project leaders should use their teams to periodically review the project and to confront project problems as they occur. Confronting and working through challenges is one of the best ways for team members to develop their skills. Additionally, teams can often spot and solve problems better than individuals working alone—even experienced project leaders. In so doing, teams get better at project work, and leaders get a double benefit—team development and good advice on project challenges.

SUCCESSFUL TEAMS ARE SATISFIED AND COMMITTED

The final criterion of team success is the extent to which team members are satisfied and committed to one another, the team, and the project on which they work. During the life of the project, satisfaction and commitment are demonstrated in the amount of effort and persistence team members make toward team goals. Also, the amount of **team cohesion**—the degree team members like each other and stick together—is a good indicator of satisfaction and commitment. After the project is over, team members may express a continued desire to work with each other and the project leader on other projects. This would indicate a high level of team satisfaction, cohesion, and commitment.

FUNDAMENTALS OF TEAM STRUCTURE

Project leaders like Leanne should consider at least six fundamental team factors when building, developing, and leading teams. Three focus on construction characteristics: team size, team composition, and team governance. The others focus more on factors that affect how team members see and deal with themselves as a team: developing a team identity, team interactions, and important components of what can be called a common "team mindset."

TEAM SIZE

Although there is no *theoretical* upper limit to the size of a team, there are real practical limits. Smaller teams seem to work better for at least two reasons. First, as teams grow in size, they tend to break down into multiple informal groups who feel more attached to one another than to the larger team or project. Second, as teams grow in size, their internal dynamics become cumbersome. They begin to experience what is known as **"process loss."**[4] As size increases, it becomes more and more difficult to coordinate actions, communicate effectively, adjust to changes, and the like. It also becomes easier to let others do the work, resulting in what economists call "free riding" and social psychologists call "social loafing." Experienced project leaders know full well, for example, that doubling the size of a project team most often does *not* double output or cut project time in half!

What is the magic number? No one can really say, and it probably depends on the nature of the work a team is doing and how well the members work together. The law of diminishing returns on team size—the decrease in productivity that inevitably comes along with an increase in team members—begins to kick in early, however. Project leaders will certainly start to see the effects of it as team size moves into the teens.[5]

TEAM COMPOSITION

Team composition refers to who should be on a project team. The chief considerations for team membership are the knowledge, skills, and abilities to do the project's work—to produce its deliverables. Quite often, these skills are technical in nature. Another set of skills team members should have are the kind of social or "people skills" needed to keep a team working together and to help connect its work with various external stakeholders. Team members who can get along and work through stressful situations, for example, are an important asset. When project tasks require contact with clients, managers in the host organization, or other important stakeholders, having the interpersonal skills to do so well can also be critical to a team's success.[6] Team members with managerial and leadership skills are also needed. Project work needs to be planned, organized, and executed in effective and efficient ways. The more team members have these kinds of skills, the more leaders can turn over project responsibilities to them.

TEAM GOVERNANCE

The amount of control a team has over its own project management is also an important factor to consider. Team control can vary a great deal. At one extreme are **manager-led teams** that have little control over their own team operations. They are told what to do and how to do it. It may well be that there are a number of ongoing teams that work for the Los Padres School District that fit this description. When they first form, project teams tend to be manager-led because the project leader plays a more directive role in laying out the project and launching project work. Manager-led teams can be quite successful in achieving whatever goals and objectives are assigned to them. As teams mature, however, they can get better at what they do and address a wider range of challenges if they can develop into self-managed work teams.

    Self-managed teams have more control over their operations. They are given their objectives, but how they achieve them is up to the team members. Leanne may well develop some of her project teams along these lines. A team whose objective is to investigate the federal regulations that are affecting the district might develop into such a team. They would be tasked, for example, to investigate and report on the regulations, how they have been implemented, and how the federal courts have interpreted them. How they would do so, however, would be left up to them as a team. To be successful, self-managed work teams need to have the knowledge, skills, abilities, and resources to manage themselves and do project work. They need the authority to make their own operational decisions, and, of course, they need commitment to project goals as well.

Self-directed and self-governing teams are two other kinds of team governance systems, but they are rarely seen in project or other organizational work. **Self-directed teams** have control over the choice of team objectives as well as team operations. Once launched, project teams are usually given their objectives as well as their required deliverables. Early in the project initiation process, however, project leaders may have some voice in establishing or defining project objectives, and they would be well advised to use it. Leanne, for example, has been given a mission and three broad objectives: identify critical issues, develop requisite information, and provide recommendations for action to the board. She should take this opportunity, however, to help define her project objectives and deliverables more specifically and have the board of supervisors endorse them.

Finally, **self-governing teams** determine their own missions and how to accomplish them. They are typically located only at the top of organizational hierarchies and are almost never found as project teams. The board of supervisors, for example, might operate as a self-governing team.[7]

TEAM IDENTITY

Effective teams also need a **team identity**.[8] Members need to see themselves as a team separate and distinct from other people and teams. Just as important, people outside the team need to see it as a team and treat it as such. That way, outsiders know where they can go to get project business done and which teams have legitimate claim over project-relevant resources.

Team identities can be developed any number of ways. "Co-locating" team members in the same physical setting will tend to foster a perception of "we-ness" among them and a perception of "they-ness" toward those outside the team. Team names also tend to foster a team identity. The "steering committee," the "Achievement Project team," and the "Upper Westside Parents' Group" are all examples of teams that may play some role in the Achievement Project. Their names help them define who they are and what they do—for themselves as well as others with whom they deal.

TEAM INTERACTIONS

Team members need to interact with one another to get project work done. The modes and styles of team interaction have taken on new importance as older forms have given way to newer ones. Traditional project teams were typically located together. Their basic form of interaction was face-to-face. Newer forms of communications and interaction have allowed the development of virtual teams.[9] Unbounded by geography, team members use a wide array of digital communications to interact with one another. With virtual teams, project leaders can tap human resources from around the world, and they can use a wide variety of project management software to help them do so. Even traditional teams working closely together now use digital communications to interact with one another more effectively.

The most potent form of interaction, however, remains face-to-face interaction for at least two reasons. First, face-to-face interaction allows for far richer forms of communication. A wider variety of nonverbal communication can occur face-to-face, for example, than can occur with most digital forms of communication. Body language, tone of voice, pauses, and the like all add to the richness of face-to-face communication. Second, face-to-face interaction facilitates the exercise of group pressure far more than digital interaction. Team members get a deeper feeling for what the team as a whole considers important when dealing with one another face-to-face.

As face-to-face interaction is replaced with other means of interaction, the team begins to lose this richness of interaction and power of physical presence. Voice-only communications like phone conferences filter out body language. E-mails filter out pauses, intonations, and a sense of what the other person is feeling. Asynchronous communications like e-mail also make it difficult to get the immediate feedback needed to keep communications and interactions accurate, effective, and efficient. Even video chat services cannot replace the power of a person's physical presence.

This does not mean that the means and modes of digital communication and virtual interactions have not added a great deal of potential to project work. They have, and as they develop, they will surely add more. Face-to-face interactions, however, will likely remain the richer and more potent form of communication, and project leaders would be wise to build in and budget for them at critical junctures in the project.

It is likely that Leanne will want to have face-to-face interactions, for example, with her own core project team and with critical stakeholder groups around the district. Initial meetings and important milestones should command face-to-face interactions as well. Certainly, as unanticipated problems arise over project goals or the appropriate means to achieve them, face-to-face interactions will allow for richer communications and a more open negotiating venue.

A Common Team Mindset

Effective teams have a common **team mindset**. By *team mindset*, I mean that team members have common ideas, views, and values about things important to the team. What constitutes appropriate and inappropriate team behavior, who should be doing what and how, and what the team is trying to achieve, for example, are all critical components of a team's common mindset. Team members may engage in different tasks, be located in different locations, or face unexpected problems. The more they share common ideas about the team and how it works, however, the more they will think and react as a cohesive, coordinated unit.[10]

Although there are a variety of different ideas that can constitute a common team mindset, three critical kinds of ideas deserve special attention: ideas about team norms, team roles, and team goals.

Norms

Norms are the rules teams develop about how their members should act—what is acceptable and what is not. Although teams can adopt norms from outside the team, most often they rise from the common expectations team members have of one another. Quite often, teams are unaware of their own norms until they are pointed out or someone violates them.

Norms are the principal means teams use to govern themselves—to hold themselves mutually accountable. Teams can control themselves to the extent that team members have clear expectations of one another and have both the means and the will to enforce those expectations.

Effective teams tend to adopt and enforce a few pivotal norms.[11] In project teams, these include norms covering the project's deliverables and how they should be produced. Norms about what constitutes proper team behavior with regard to the project and to one another are other kinds of critical norms that should be considered.

Like any project leader, Leanne should address pivotal project norms early in the life of her project. Giving key norms explicit attention will help her team establish the policies and procedures needed for its own command and control system.

Roles

A defining characteristic of any team is that its members do different tasks. To be successful, the results or output of those tasks must come together into a coherent product or service. For all this to happen, team members must perform different roles that fit together well.

Team **roles** are like roles in a play. They are the behaviors team members must perform for the team to have a successful "production." The team's **"task roles"** attend to the production of the project's products and services. **"Maintenance,"** "socio-emotional," or **"people roles"** attend to keeping everyone working together well. Finally, "managerial" or **"leadership roles"** attend to the management and organizational needs of the project and to keeping it on track. Unlike roles in a play, team roles are not defined by scriptwriters and clarified by directors. Team roles arise from the often unspoken expectations of team members themselves.

When a team works well together, its members perform the roles that are needed, when they are needed, and in ways that are needed. Although this is easy to say, it is often difficult to accomplish for a number of reasons. First, important roles are often overlooked. This is less of a problem with task roles because the project's objectives and work breakdown structure tend to focus attention on them. Leadership and managerial roles, however, tend to get less attention. What the leader expects from the team and what the team can expect from the leader are role elements that often go unexpressed. The roles leaders will play in decision making, providing close or loose supervision, providing training, and the like are generally ignored until problems arise. "People" roles are the most overlooked. Little express attention is paid to what is expected in terms of cooperating, handling conflict, facilitating participation, addressing what constitutes appropriate team citizenship, and the like until conflicts demand attention.

A second problem with proper role play is that different people have different expectations of role holders. Almost always, this leads to increases in conflict and losses in team performance. The different and conflicting expectations experienced by project leaders are a case in point. When teams first come together, their members typically have very different preferences and expectations of the project manager. So do clients, managers in the host organization, and other external stakeholders. In a similar way, team members have differing expectations of one another that often cause problems in role performance.

The third problem in role performance arises when role holders do not have the full range of knowledge, skills, and abilities to perform their roles well. Generally, a fair amount of attention is given to the skills needed to perform the task roles of a project. Far less attention is usually given to the skills needed to perform people roles and, surprisingly, leadership roles well.

Early in the life cycle of any new project, team members need to develop a common understanding of the important roles that need to be played in the project, how they are to be played, and who will play them. This can be done in at least two ways. First, time can be set aside to discuss critical team roles as a team topic in itself. What the team can expect from its leader and from one another are two role topics that warrant discussion early in any project. Second, roles themselves should be considered a legitimate and important topic to address as problems with roles—team member expectations of one another—emerge. When roles are given early and continuing attention as needed, role performance will increase along with project performance.

Goals

A common understanding about the overall purpose of the project and its specific deliverables is one of the most important factors in a team's success. **Goals** give common direction to a team. The more specific the goals, the more specific the direction.

The goal specification process in project management attends well to this issue (see Chapter 2). Laying out how the project's mission, objectives, deliverables, and task objectives relate to one another—and what is needed to produce them—all combine to provide a good **goal structure** to a project. The next need, then, is for the project team to develop a common understanding of the goal structure and how the product of their work fits into it. Meetings early in the project cycle covering the goal structure and how it was produced will go a long way toward producing the common understanding of project goals needed for project work.

TEAM DEVELOPMENT

Project teams form anew with each new project. At first, the team is simply a collection of individuals in a project group. For these groups to become project teams, they need to go through a process of team development.[12] Team development has been studied from a variety of perspectives, but one has received the most attention: the "stage model" of team development developed by Tuckman and Jensen.[13] This model breaks the development of teams into five stages: forming, storming, norming, performing, and adjourning. Project leaders can help their teams develop more quickly when they are aware of these stages and the team's needs in each phase.

FORMING

When project groups are first **forming,** their members are unclear about the goals and priorities of the project ahead and the roles they will play. As with many first introductions, members also tend to be polite and cautious and to monitor their comments and behaviors. They tend to go along with most of what is being said as they try to feel one another out. If they have disagreements or concerns, they tend to hold back on their comments.

At this early stage, the team needs to have the project's goals clarified as well as the basic plans to achieve them. Members will also want to know what task roles they will play and how they are expected to play them. This is a good time, too, to address some of the more important, pivotal norms that will be used to govern project behaviors.

The cautious politeness that characterizes the forming stage has at least two other implications for project leadership. The first is that most team members tend to defer to those who are more dominant. Some project members may use this opportunity to assert their own ideas and begin to take over project discussions and decision making. Project leadership is a central concern to the team at this stage, and although participation is welcomed, the project leader needs to establish command of the project team from the very beginning. This is accomplished by demonstrating an in-depth knowledge of the project and its needs, a command of team process, and a comfortable assumption of one's own project authority.

A second implication for leadership in the forming stage is that project leaders often find that team members will tend to agree with almost anything they say. Leaders should be aware, however, that this "silent affirmation" might be due to members simply holding back, as is characteristic of this stage. The stresses and strains of the project itself may soon call into question early work in team development.

STORMING

The **storming** stage is characterized by open or covert conflict over project issues. The term *storming* tends to evoke mental images of thunder and lightning. Some teams may exhibit this kind of conflict, but most do not. Teams go through a storming stage simply because different people have different ideas about the project and how it should be run. These differences begin to emerge once the honeymoon of the forming stage is over and people feel freer to express their opinions.

One common response to differing ideas among team members is to share them with one or two others who may hold similar views. In this way, larger project teams break into smaller, informal subgroups whose members tend to see things the same way but differently from other subgroups. Left unaddressed for too long, disagreements between subgroups can erupt into the kind of open conflict for which this stage is named. At this point, struggles for power can emerge, communications can suffer, and project work can slow down and become uncoordinated.

Project leaders should not be surprised when disagreements emerge within the team. In fact, they should expect them. If they remain hidden, the leader may even want to seek them out for at least two reasons. First, different views can bring with them good ideas about the project and how it might be run. Although snap decisions about project changes should be avoided, leaders should be open to new and better ways to run the project.[14] Second, when disagreements are found, they are more easily resolved earlier rather than later in the project. Although team members may disagree about one or another aspect of the project, most simply want their ideas considered and resolved. The team tends to look to the project leader to play the lead role in resolving differences, and members will generally defer to the leader if they believe their views have been given due consideration.[15]

NORMING

Norming is the stage in which project members come to understand and accept the norms of the project, its goals, and one another's roles. Although everyone may not be in 100% agreement with all project particulars, the team has come to a common understanding and acceptance of the project and how it is to be run. Noticeable characteristics of this stage are team cohesion and commitment to the project and its objectives.

PERFORMING

The **performing** stage is when the team begins to act like a team. Their work is well coordinated, and they have learned to deal with problems productively as they arise. Decisions about project work are given to those best able to make them and project work to those best skilled to do it.

As the team moves through the norming and performing stages, less supervision is needed because the team itself is taking on some important elements of the leadership role. This kind of team maturity means that the team can assume most, if not all, of the responsibilities of a self-managed work team. This does not mean that project leaders can ignore the project team or abdicate their leadership role. Project leaders continue to monitor project work, of course, so that no surprises occur. It does mean, however, that project leaders can turn more of their attention to other matters vital to the project, such as communicating with stakeholders, planning, forecasting problems, and adapting to change.

ADJOURNING

All project work ends, and project members may leave earlier than project completion if their contributions are complete. **Adjourning** is a process that should command the project leader's attention as well. The contributions of project members should be recognized so that project members can feel good about their work. Debriefs or after-action reviews should also be conducted, either formally or informally, to wrap up the lessons learned from the project.[16]

Wise project leaders will also take note of those members who were particularly valuable to the project and who went above and beyond the call of duty. Special rewards and thanks should be given to them. Word gets around about leaders who reward good work—and those who ignore it. Leaders should also keep track of particularly good personnel for the next project that may need their skills.

SUMMARY

The term *team* has been used to refer to many different kinds of groups. In this chapter, we use Katzenbach and Smith's characterization.[17] A team is a small number of people with complementary skills who are committed to a common purpose, a common set of performance goals, and a common approach for which they hold themselves mutually accountable.

There are at least three criteria to assess team success. First and foremost, successful teams deliver the goods to their clients—on time, on budget, and according to specification. Project leaders need to be aware, however, that many stakeholders are involved in determining project success, and their views need attention as well. Second, successful teams also get better at what they do—they develop into better teams and team members. Attention to team development pays off even when dealing with temporary project teams. Finally, successful teams are committed to the project, to one another, and to their leader.

Teams have a number of characteristics that should be considered when building, developing, and leading them. The first is team size. Smaller teams tend to do better than larger teams. Larger teams suffer process losses and tend to break down into smaller groups. A second consideration is the knowledge, skills, and abilities of those who compose the team. Skills to do the task work, skills needed to attend to people issues, and managerial and leadership skills are all needed in project work. A third important issue is team governance. Although project teams may start out as manager-led teams, more productive teams evolve into self-managed work teams with autonomy and control over their own operations as they pursue project objectives. A fourth factor to consider is that teams need an identity of their own. They need to have definite boundaries and to be seen as a team both by themselves and by others. A fifth issue to consider is how the team will interact with one another. Digital communications can offer a great deal to project work. Face-to-face interactions, however, provide the richest form of communication and provide the team with more power over its members. Face-to-face interactions are particularly helpful at crucial junctures of a project like at its initiation, at important milestones, and when confronting important problems. A final consideration is that teams need to develop a common team mindset—common ideas and a common understanding of the team, its norms, its roles, and its goals. Successful teams often use a few pivotal norms to hold themselves accountable to one another and to the project. Members of successful project teams also perform their roles well. These include task, people, and leadership roles. Common problems that undermine good role performance include not developing important roles that need to be played; different team members having different expectations of a person's role; and not having the knowledge, skills, or abilities to play one's role well. The goals of successful teams are also understood and shared by everyone on the team. One way to develop a common understanding of team norms, roles, and goals is to openly discuss them early in a project and to view their discussion as legitimate throughout the project as the need arises.

Teams develop through different stages—forming, storming, norming, performing, and adjourning. The forming stage is characterized by polite restraint on the part of team members who may be strangers to one another. At this stage, the team is uncertain about the goals of the team and the roles they will play in it. They are also unsure about how the team will be led. These and similar issues of concern need to be addressed early in a project. Although project leaders may witness a fair amount of silent agreement of their leadership at this early stage of development, they should be aware that this may be due to team members simply holding back comments, which is characteristic of this stage.

The storming stage is characterized by open or covert conflict over project issues. This stage emerges because different people have different ideas about the project. Project leaders should not be surprised or angry when such differences arise. Some ideas might be used to make the project better, and in any event, differences are more productively addressed early rather than later in the project cycle. Most team members want project differences resolved and look to the project leader to do so. They will tend to defer to the leader if they believe that their views are given due consideration.

The norming stage is when the project team has come to understand, accept, and commit to the norms, roles, and goals of a project. Noticeable characteristics are team cohesion and commitment to the project. The performing stage is when the project team functions as a team, performing project work in a well-coordinated fashion, making effective and productive decisions, and dealing with team issues as they arise. As teams move through the norming and performing stages, they can assume more and more of the responsibilities of a self-managed work team, allowing project leaders to spend more time on their other leadership responsibilities.

Adjourning is the stage when the project ends. This is the time for looking back and taking stock of the project—to take note and record important lessons learned. Project leaders do well to recognize good performance and keep track of productive project personnel for future projects.

REVIEW QUESTIONS

1. How does the chapter define a team?

   a. How do the components relate to team effectiveness?

2. Identify and discuss the criteria for team success.

   a. Give a concrete example of each criterion in terms of a project.

3. Six factors were identified as fundamentals of team structure that play key roles in the building, development, and leading of teams.

   a. Identify and discuss the effects of each factor.

   b. With regard to ideology, discuss the effects of team norms, roles, and goals and some of the problems encountered with each of them. With each, present how a project leader might address those problems.

4. Identify and characterize the stages of development a team goes through from first coming together to full maturity.

   a. What, if any, are the needs that leaders should address at each stage of development?

EXERCISES

1. Identify one or two of the best and one or two of the worst school or work teams on which you served as a member.

    a. Identify the top three to five factors that made the team the best or the worst in terms of your experience.

    b. To what extent do those factors coincide with issues covered in this chapter?

    c. How do the factors you have identified add to the issues covered?

    d. If you were the leader of the worst teams with full authority over them, what would be the top 10 things you would do to ensure their success?

2. Using the best and worst teams identified previously, develop a profile of each team using Table 6.1: "Comparison Issues for Best and Worst Teams."

    a. Use the criteria of team success in your profile.

    b. Review the fundamentals of team structure in your profile.

    c. Review the stages of team development and consider the extent to which the team matured and the stages through which it progressed. What needs at each stage were addressed or ignored? What was the effect?

Table 6.1   Comparison Issues for Best and Worst Teams

	Best #1	*Best #2*	*Worst #1*	*Worst #2*
Success Criteria				
Goal accomplishment				
Development				
Satisfaction				
Team Structure				
Team size				
Composition				
Governance				
Interactions				
Team norms				
Team roles				
Team goals				
Team Development				
Forming				
Storming				
Norming				
Performing				
Adjourning				

3. You have just been made leader of a project of your own choosing.

   a. Think through and describe the project.

   b. Present what you would do to help pull together, develop, and lead your team. Pay particular attention to team and project needs in the early stages of team development and how you would respond to them.

4. If you are a member of a class team, discuss its norms, roles, and goals. Use this chapter as a starting point for your discussion. Work toward common agreement about a few pivotal norms with which all can agree, important roles and how and who should play them, and the concrete deliverables your team will produce.

ENDNOTES

1. Katzenbach, J. R., & Smith, D. K. (1993, March/April). The discipline of teams. *Harvard Business Review, 71,* 111–120.

2. Hackman, J. R. (2002). *Leading teams: Setting the stage for great performances.* Boston, MA: Harvard Business School Press. Goodman, D. S., Ravlin, E., & Schminke, M. (1987). Understanding groups in organizations. In L. L. Cummings & B. Staw (Eds.), *Research in organizational behavior* (Vol. 9, pp. 121–173). Greenwich, CT: JAI.

3. I am aware of many project leaders who have the reputation of being "hard drivers" but who have no difficulty recruiting willing project members because members know these leaders will attend to their development as well as to the project's deliverables.

4. Steiner, I. D. (1972). *Group process and productivity.* New York, NY: Academic Press.

5. Of course, projects can include hundreds of people working on any number of jobs. Project leaders, however, would do well to break down project work so those hundreds of people can be formed into a number of smaller teams. In these cases, the project leader is really leading an organization of teams with its own demands.

6. I know of a number of project leaders who have made serious mistakes in this regard. One, for example, made the decision to transfer a particularly bothersome team member offsite to serve as liaison to the client just to get rid of him. Needless to say, this turned out to be a serious error.

7. These governance examples are from: Hackman, J. R. (1987). The design of work teams. In J. W. Lorsch (Ed.), *Handbook of organizational behavior* (pp. 315–342). Upper Saddle River, NJ: Prentice Hall.

8. Hackman (2002).

9. Cascio, W. (2000). Managing a virtual workplace. *Academy of Management Executive, 14*(2), 81–90. Townsend, A. M., DeMarie, S. M., & Hendricson, A. R. (1998). Virtual teams: Technology and the workplace of the future. *Academy of Management Executive, 12*(3), 17–29.

10. The notion of a "group mind" has received more attention in recent years. See, for example: Austin, J. (2003). Transactive memory in organizational groups: The effects of content, consensus, specialization, and accuracy on group performance. *Journal of Applied Psychology*, 88, 866–878. Gibson, C. (2001). From knowledge accumulation to accommodation: Cycles of collective cognition in work groups. *Journal of Organizational Behavior*, 22, 121–134. Marks, M. A., Burke, C. S., Sabella, M. J., & Zaccaro, S. J. (2002). The impact of cross-training on team effectiveness. *Journal of Applied Psychology*, 87, 3–13.

11. Hackman (2002).

12. More experienced project personnel take far less time to do so than those new to project work.

13. The following discussion is based on: Tuckman, B. W., & Jensen, M. A. C. (1977). Stages of small group development revisited. *Group and Organization Studies*, 2, 419–428. This discussion also includes information from: Obert, S. L. (1978). *The development of organizational task groups* (PhD dissertation, Case Western Reserve University), as cited in: Cohen, A. R., Fink, S. L., Gadon, H., & Willits, R. D. (1984). *Effective behavior in organizations*. Homewood, IL: Irwin.

14. Leaders need to carefully consider the longer term consequences of ideas brought to them. Project members quite often do not have the broader project picture held by the project leader. Leaders need to make changes very carefully with full consideration given to effects on the project schedule, budget, and deliverables as well as on relevant stakeholders.

15. Although not common, some project members may continue to engage in destructive and disruptive conflict for reasons of their own. The project leader should seek to solidify the rest of the project team in the face of such opposition, and then move to remove it if it cannot be constructively resolved.

16. After-action reviews should not be relegated to the closing phase of projects. At most, if not all milestones, it is a good idea to look back to see if there are any lessons to be learned for the rest of the project. We discussed this in relation to the management of risk in Chapter 5.

17. Katzenbach & Smith (1993).

KEY TERMS

Adjourning: the final stage of team development when all project work ends or when project members leave earlier than project completion if their contributions are complete.

Forming: the first stage of team development when team members are unclear about the goals and priorities of the project ahead and the roles they will play.

Goal Structure: how the project's mission, objectives, and deliverables and the task objectives are related to each other and what is needed to produce them.

Goals: a common direction for the team, a common understanding about the overall purpose of the project and its specific deliverables.

Leadership Roles: leadership behaviors team members must perform to keep the team controlled and organized.

Manager-Led Teams: teams who have little control over their own team operations. They are told what to do and how to do it.

Norming: the stage of team development in which project members come to understand and accept the norms of the project, its goals, and one another's roles.

Norms: rules teams develop about how their members should act—what is acceptable and what is not.

People Roles: people-oriented behaviors team members must perform to keep the team working together well.

Performing: the stage of team development when the team begins to act like a team.

Process Loss: when it becomes more and more difficult to coordinate actions, communicate effectively, and adjust to changes and easier to let others do the work as team size increases.

Roles: the behaviors team members must perform for the team to be successful. These include task, people, and leadership roles. Roles rise from the expectations team members have of one another.

Self-Directed Teams: teams who have control over the choice of team objectives as well as team operations.

Self-Governing Teams: teams who determine their own missions and how to accomplish them.

Self-Managed Teams: teams who have more control over their operations. They are given their objectives, but how they achieve them is up to the team members.

Storming: the stage of team development that is characterized by open or covert conflict over project issues.

Synergy: when a team produces more than the sum of individual team contributions.

Task Roles: task behaviors team members must perform for the team to be successful in the development of deliverables.

Team: a small number of people with complementary skills who are committed to a common purpose, a common set of performance goals, and a common approach for which they hold themselves mutually accountable.

Team Cohesion: the degree to which team members like one another and stick together.

Team Identity: the degree to which team members see themselves as separate and distinct from other people and teams.

Team Mindset: the common values, perspectives, and ideas that team members have about things important to the team.

The Project Team's Environment

INTRODUCTION

THE ACHIEVEMENT PROJECT

In Chapter 6, we met Leanne Phillips. She works for the Los Padres School District and was charged by the board of supervisors to lead an important project. Changes in federal regulations threatened the funding received by the district. A small but sizable percentage of students were not meeting the achievement levels mandated by the regulations. The board charged Leanne with identifying the most critical issues involved in the problem, developing the information they would need to understand and address those issues, and making recommendations about courses of action the board should take.

It wasn't long before word got out about the project. In fact, the "Achievement Project" was the name the local newspaper gave it, and the local TV and radio news programs picked it up. In a matter of just 2 days, Leanne was receiving dozens of calls and more than 30 e-mails each day from people who were interested—and wanted to have a say—in the Achievement Project. Teachers, principals, board members, and the presidents of various parent-teacher association chapters in the district were all calling her. So, too, were salespeople with a wide variety of products for at-risk students. The legal counsel for the district was also in touch with her, as were regulators from the state's department of education. Leanne was only 3 days into the project, and all these people were already making demands and competing for her attention. She knew, as well, that this was only the beginning. Many more people would express interest in the project before it was over.

OVERVIEW OF CHAPTER

Leanne is experiencing a much larger dose of what most project leaders experience. Projects never exist in isolation. They are always connected to a network of people and organizations—stakeholders—who are affected by them in some way and who want some say in how they are run or what they will produce. Project leaders need to be able to identify these important stakeholders and manage their interactions with the project.

This chapter focuses on project stakeholders and how to work with them. We first examine different kinds of stakeholders, some of the key things they desire, and how project leaders might respond to them. We then turn our attention to look at the project environment more strategically. Project leaders play a critical role in managing the external networks of their project's stakeholders. Finally, we address what those networks look like, the role project leaders need to play in them, and how to develop and maintain those networks.

STAKEHOLDERS

Stakeholders are those people, organizational units, and institutions that have a vested interest in the conduct and outcome of the project and can affect it in some way. The most critical stakeholders are those who are most affected by the project and those who have the most say in how it is run and what it produces. Balancing the interests, desires, and needs of so diverse a group is a challenge for any project leader.

Each project will have its own unique profile of stakeholders, but we will examine some of the more common ones in this section. We look first at three particularly important stakeholders: project clients, the managers of the organization that hosts the project, and the project team. For various reasons, these stakeholders usually have a great deal of say in how a project is set up and conducted. We then examine external and internal resource suppliers. Projects depend on others for resources, and so they, too, can affect the project. We give attention next to regulators. Projects often have to meet regulatory standards, so leaders need to work with those who enforce them. Many projects are intended to benefit others after the project itself is completed. These end users of the project need to be addressed as well. Additionally, any implementers—those who may be tasked with executing project recommendations—should be kept in mind throughout the project as partners in the next step of the process. Finally, we address a set of stakeholders who are often ignored in the project management literature but who are very important: political players—the informal supporters and opponents with whom projects often deal.

PROJECT CLIENTS

Project **clients** are those for whom the project is being conducted as well as the ultimate source of resources for the project. The reason why clients sponsor a project at all is because they want it to address some set of their needs. Project leaders usually work with clients throughout the project, but their services often differ at the beginning of, during, and at the closing of projects.

At the beginning of projects, leaders must often help clients clarify their needs in terms of project objectives and concrete deliverables. Chapter 2 is largely dedicated to this all-important activity, but one key point is worth repeating. Clients often have only vague ideas about their needs and how a project might address them in terms of concrete products and services. Helping clients identify these project specifics is one of the most important services project leaders provide their clients and their own project teams. The process of determining specific project deliverables can occur quickly and easily, or, as is likely in Leanne's case, it can take quite a bit of effort. It is critical, however, that a project charter—as discussed in Chapter 2, with deliverables, budget, and a timeline spelled out—be developed and agreed to by the client, the host organization, and the project leader.

During the course of the project, clients will often want assurances that the project is proceeding as planned. This need is generally best met by structuring milestones into the project at which time progress is noted, formal reports are made, and important issues are discussed. These reporting events require effort, resources, and time and should be included in the project's planning and budgeting. This is not to say, however, that client contact can or should be strictly limited to these events. Some clients can be rather high-maintenance, and in any event, project leaders will want to keep their clients appropriately informed about important developments. Every effort should be made, however, to buffer the project team from undue disturbances in their work.

The end of a project is signaled by the delivery of the project's final products and services to the client. Many project leaders develop checklists of project deliverables and expectations so they can work through them with clients at this time. Tied to the initial specifications of project deliverables in the project charter, these can be useful tools for focusing attention on key closing elements. Often, additional work may be required to fully close down a project and satisfy a client. Project leaders need to be aware of this possibility and incorporate postdelivery work into the project plan and budget.

The project's aim is, after all, to meet or exceed the client's expectations. The key concept, here, is *expectations*. From the initial specification of project deliverables to the project's conclusion, the project leader needs to keep track of and manage those expectations. During the course of a project, for example, clients may get other ideas for products and services they would like. Project leaders will generally want to work with clients to show how such changes—known as "**scope creep**" because the scope of the project slowly begins to expand—will require additional time and resources. This usually helps refocus the client's attention on the originally agreed-upon deliverables. The changes, then, can be discussed in terms of follow-up projects.

As you can see, working with clients can be a challenge. Many project leaders feel uncomfortable meeting and establishing working relationships with new people. Nevertheless, the client plays too many critical roles in the project to be ignored.

HOST ORGANIZATION MANAGEMENT

Host organization management—higher level managers within the organization where the project is conducted—are also significant stakeholders. The project leader's direct supervisor is one of the most significant of those. In project and matrix organizations, projects are undertaken as the company's business. In such cases, higher management's aims are that projects remain profitable and be conducted within the operating budget and other constraints established for project work.

Often, as in the case of the Achievement Project, projects are undertaken for the benefit of the organization itself. In these cases, higher management also plays the role of an outside client and can pose the same kinds of challenges presented by clients.

In all cases, project leaders will want their direct supervisors and higher management to support and champion the projects they lead: to help make sure that the project gets the resources it needs and run interference for the project as it progresses though its life cycle.

For its part, management wants to know that the project is proceeding as planned. Structured progress reports similar to those given to clients can serve this need.[1] Unexpected problems of strategic importance need to be brought to management's attention quickly, along with options about how to address them. In general, however, higher management expects project leaders to handle routine problems themselves.

THE PROJECT TEAM

Projects are unique endeavors and require a great deal of problem solving to produce the products or services required. Most often, projects work under strict timelines and budgets. In addition, project personnel often have organizational commitments other than the project itself. All of these characteristics can combine to produce a fair amount of stress on **project teams**—the group of people who are actually carrying out project activities.

Project teams want to be able to do the project—to bring it to a successful conclusion. Initially, teams want to clearly understand the project and how it is to be done. Toward these ends, leaders need to present the team with clear project objectives and a clear, actionable plan to achieve them. The team also needs the resources required for the project. The most important of these is the composition of the team itself. The members need to possess the knowledge, skills, and abilities required by the project. During the conduct of the project, resources need to arrive according to specifications and when needed.[2]

As project teams conduct the project, they need to be protected from unnecessary outside pressures that will distract them. Projects have many stakeholders with varied interests, and project leaders need to buffer their teams while they themselves develop the stakeholder linkages appropriate to the team's work.

Finally, project members do not want to be overcommitted. Project leaders need to be aware of and sensitive to the demands placed on members of their team. In addition to careful scheduling, leaders should work with those outside the project who have a legitimate claim on project personnel to help clear their schedules.

EXTERNAL SUPPLIERS

External suppliers are those outside the organization who provide project resources. These resources are often critical to project success and need to arrive on time, as budgeted, and according to specifications. It is not uncommon to find, however, that external suppliers are less motivated by these needs than the project leader. Contrary to popular belief, just because something is paid for does not mean that the project will get what it needs when planned.

Project leaders should do all they can to ensure timely delivery of critical and unique resources. This can be done by developing contracts with external suppliers and by scheduling lead times into delivery schedules. As delivery times come near, project personnel can check to make sure everything is going according to schedule. It is a good idea, too, for project leaders to establish relationships with their critical vendors. If at all possible, leaders should get to know at least one contact person who can pull strings to make things happen when problems arise.

INTERNAL SUPPLIERS

Internal suppliers are those within the host organization who supply the project with resources. Personnel and information are the most common resources provided, but things like office space, the loan of equipment, and even raw material might be provided as well.

Even in project organizations where personnel are routinely assigned to projects, conflicts can emerge over who gets assigned, when, and for how long. In more traditional organizations in which others are imposed on to provide help to a project, the conflict potential is even higher. Providing resources to others often produces problems of scheduling, conflicts between requests from other projects, and the day-to-day demands pressing on the supplier's own unit. Project leaders need to be as sensitive as possible to these issues.

It is important for project leaders to work as closely as they can with the project's internal suppliers. They should strive to give them as much lead time as possible so supplying units can work around the loss. If resources are needed on a continuing basis, developing a more personal relationship can help as well. In all cases, project leaders should be sure to thank those within the organization who provide resources to the project. A good word to higher management about how much they helped the project would be appreciated as well.

If, despite all good efforts, resources are still being withheld, project leaders may have to take alternative actions. As a last resort, project managers can ask higher management to address the resource problem. Keep in mind, however, that higher management generally prefers project leaders to handle these matters. Also, using higher management tends to cost serious political capital, and it rarely wins friends from the supplying unit.

REGULATORS

Projects often have to meet certain levels of quality in either the products and services the project delivers or in the ways the project itself is conducted. Regulators are the people who make sure projects achieve those levels of quality.

External regulators are usually independent organizations or agencies with formal authority to check up on project deliverables or the conduct of projects. Building inspectors, for example, approve or disapprove the structural requirements of building construction. Inspectors from the Occupational Safety and Health Administration make sure the physical welfare of project workers is being addressed. **Internal regulators** work for the host organization and generally attend to the conduct of the project (e.g., internal auditors and the contracts office). State, federal, and district regulators will play these external and internal regulatory roles in Leanne's project.

To be truly effective, regulators must be independent of the project and its organizational line of authority. Moreover, regulators are often required to limit their interactions with those whom they regulate to maintain their objectivity. When regulators find that project work is out of compliance, for example, they may have the authority to shut down the project, but they may not be allowed to suggest changes. All these aspects of the regulatory relationship make working with regulators something of a challenge.[3]

Project leaders should pay extra attention, then, to regulatory requirements in the planning, budgeting, and execution stages of any project. As the risks of regulatory failure rise in a project, leaders may consider early, preliminary inspections or the use of outside consultants with regulatory experience to review the project and its conduct as needed.

END USERS AND IMPLEMENTERS

Projects are often designed to benefit others in addition to the sponsoring client. Leanne's project is only one example. Her project's end users—those who will ultimately use or benefit from the project—are the at-risk students with low achievement scores. Like many projects, Leanne's project will end before these ultimate users will make use of her work. Although the project's recommendations will hopefully benefit these students, the Achievement Project itself will not implement the recommendations. Even so, such projects should be planned and executed with these stakeholders in mind.[4]

Other postproject stakeholders are those who will carry out the project's recommendations—implementers. For a variety of obvious reasons, the project team is often well suited to implement the products and services they have produced. Clients frequently require initial implementation as part of the project with a period of product and service maintenance thereafter. Other projects, however, recommend postproject actions and rely on others to implement them. In the Achievement Project, for example, the teachers of the at-risk students and the principals of the schools they attend will play implementing roles for those recommendations approved by the board. Although Leanne's team may not implement the project's recommendations, they can make better, more action-oriented recommendations by knowing more about the challenges faced and the resources needed by those who will implement it. Project leaders need to plan for and have their projects funded to produce the kinds of deliverables that are useful to postproject stakeholders. In addition, project teams often come across resources and material that may be useful to implementers. Collecting or cataloging these kinds of resources can be a low-cost, high-value-added addition to a project.

POLITICAL PLAYERS

Finally, the project leader needs to be aware of another kind of stakeholder: political players within the host organization. **Political players** are those who use their influence to actively support or oppose the project based on their own interests and aims. It has long been known that once you step into a leadership role, you are also stepping into a political arena where competing interests often come into conflict.[5] Projects, in particular, can increase political concerns. Projects, after all, are designed to make things happen—to create and put into place something new. This means change—change caused by the simple conduct of the project as well as the change envisioned by the goals of the project itself. Any change will have supporters and opponents. Rarely mentioned in the project management literature are the political stakeholders who are likely to emerge with the conduct of almost any project.

Project supporters and opponents can often be identified by asking a simple question: "Who will benefit and who will lose by the conduct and completion of this project?" The recommendations made by the Achievement Project, for example, may well benefit some in the school district's organization and cause loss to others. The same may be true of some stakeholders external to the district's organization. These will form part of the possible pool of political supporters and opponents of the project.

Some opponents are not opposed to the outcomes of the project as such, but to its imposition on their operations. Although an organizational unit in the organization may be ordered to help the project in some aspect of its work, for example, those in the unit may actively resist that aid for any of a number of reasons.

Unfortunately, organizational politics may also play a role in the larger context of a project. The success or failure of a project may affect the political fortunes of not only its leader but also others in the organization. The extent to which a project is successful, for example, may mean that its leader will rise in the organization while others do not.

Although projects may have their opponents, so, too, do they have their supporters. Clients and those in upper management should be major supporters. The project leader's direct supervisor should be one of the project's key champions. Keeping one's supervisors up to date on the project's progress and demonstrating one's ability to handle the problems that always arise will help keep the support one needs. There are likely other supporters of a project as well. It pays to stop by and let them know how things are going from time to time. Project leaders sometimes have a tendency to call on their supporters only when they need them. It is also a good idea to call on them when things are going well and take the opportunity to thank them for their continuing support.

It is always a good idea to give some thought to the political side of a project. If its political potential is high—as it is with the Achievement Project—identifying and reaching out to supporters as early as possible is a good idea. Their thoughts on the political side of the project can help leaders in the planning and conduct of a politically sensitive project. Establishing relationships early with supporters, identifying likely detractors, and planning when support will be needed is an unfortunate but often necessary side of successful project leadership.

DEVELOPING AND USING PROJECT NETWORKS

The previous section makes clear that projects never exist in isolation. They are surrounded by many stakeholders who will affect the conduct of the project and determine its success or failure. Being able to work in this larger network of stakeholders is one of the more important assets leaders can bring to their projects.[6] That asset has come to be called *social capital*.[7] In this section, we examine first what social capital is and then address how leaders can develop social capital in project work.

THE NATURE OF SOCIAL CAPITAL

The term "**capital**" is used by economists to refer to any asset that can be employed to produce wealth. Buildings and equipment used to manufacture products, for example, are capital assets. **Human capital** is composed of the knowledge, skills, and abilities of a person that can be used to produce things of value such as deliverables from project tasks. **Social capital** comes from a person's connections to others. It is the value someone has because he or she can tap into various social networks to get the resources needed for a job or to help coordinate, assist, or run interference for a project. A project leader's social capital, then, is his or her ability to use the resources of others in the furtherance of project work.

We all know others we can turn to when we are in need of help, and, in turn, we often provide our help to them. That is what social capital really is all about. Some project leaders, however, have far more social capital, and more project-relevant social capital, than others. Consider, for example, Figures 7.1, 7.2, and 7.3.[8] All these figures show graphical representations of different social networks in the Achievement Project. Figure 7.1 shows the social network of Leanne's principal, seven-member project team. This team is responsible for most of the project's work. In the graph, each circle represents a team member and each line represents a strong tie that binds one member to another. This team appears to be a pretty cohesive one. Each member has strong ties to most all the other members and, no doubt, can turn to them for help.

Figure 7.2 represents the social network of the larger Achievement Project organization. In addition to the principal project team, there are two others. One two-person team works on regulatory issues as needed. The other three-member team works on reviewing the records of at-risk students in the district. The student records team does not appear to be as cohesive as the principal project team because two of its members are not tied very well to one another, although both are tied to what appears to be a formal or informal team leader. Leanne has ties to all the teams. In the social network of the Achievement Project, then, Leanne has the most social capital. She can call on all the project teams for project work and support, whereas members of each team can call only on themselves. Leanne's position in this kind of social network is what one would expect of a project leader.

Figure 7.3 shows the Achievement Project organization in relation to some of its key stakeholders in its larger environment. One key stakeholder, of course, is the board of supervisors. Leanne reports to them, and they depend on her to lead the Achievement Project organization. Two other stakeholder groups are the special education teachers and the principals' group. The special education teachers will have to implement and carry through some of the recommendations of the Achievement Project. The school principals will be responsible for overseeing the implementation of those recommendations and for the students' achievements, and they will need to report to the board about the progress of the Achievement Program.

A few things are important to note in Figure 7.3. First, Leanne is tied to all stakeholder groups. This means she has some measure of access to these stakeholder groups, and to the extent she can enlist their aid and support, she has social capital because of those ties. Second, although the members of the various stakeholder groups are not closely tied to one another, at least one member in each has the most ties to all the others. That fact makes the member relatively more influential in that stakeholder group. Finally, Leanne's ties to each group are through its more influential member. That provides her with more social capital than if her ties were with less influential members.

Although some of a project leader's ties to others in this extended network may be very strong, many may be weak but quite serviceable ties. Strong ties come from constant interaction, day in and day out, over a whole host of issues important to a relationship. These kinds of ties make up strong teams. Weak ties are more like working relationships. Hopefully friendly, they tend to center on the exchange of resources each member of the network seeks from the others. As these relationships become stronger, the parties become more committed to them. Project success is based a great deal on the social capital of project members. Most often, this centers on the social capital of project leaders based on their position in the larger project network and their ability to use the ties they have developed.

Figure 7.1   The Social Network of Leanne Phillips's Principal Project Team

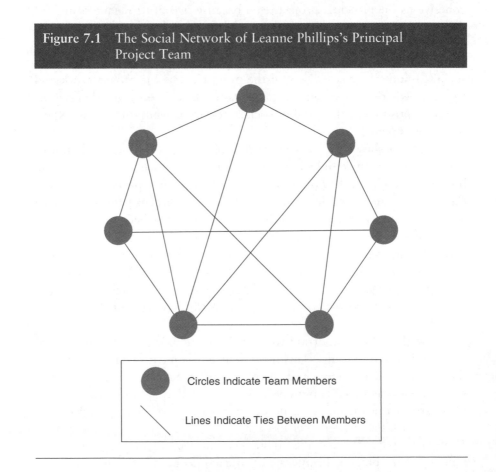

Circles Indicate Team Members

Lines Indicate Ties Between Members

Figure 7.2   The Social Network of the Achievement Project Organization

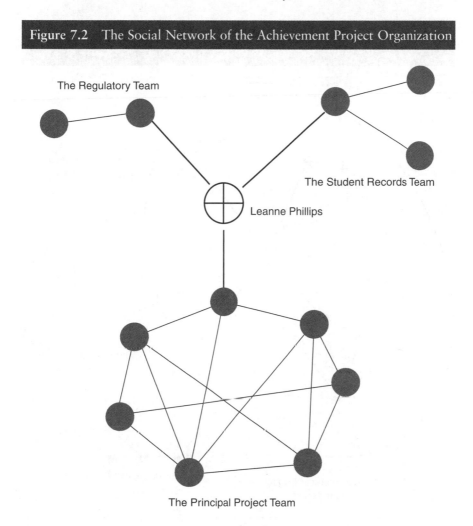

The Regulatory Team

The Student Records Team

Leanne Phillips

The Principal Project Team

DEVELOPING SOCIAL CAPITAL

Social capital is produced by developing relationships with people who have the resources and influence needed for project success. In the early project planning stage, leaders need to identify all those stakeholders who will play important decision-making and resource-sharing roles for the project. Once identified, project leaders need to self-consciously set up plans to talk at length with these stakeholders about the project.

Initial interactions are best done face-to-face and one-on-one. These kinds of one-on-one meetings allow for more candid conversations and

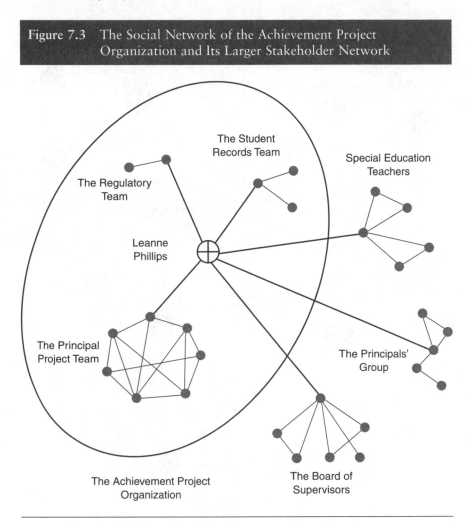

Figure 7.3   The Social Network of the Achievement Project
Organization and Its Larger Stakeholder Network

richer communication. The project leader's agenda includes assessing the
stakeholder's interests in the project, his or her likely influence over the
project, and the true role he or she will seek to play in it. Active listening is
a key skill to employ in these meetings. A great deal can be learned, for
example, by taking note of the questions stakeholders ask. Their questions
reveal their interests, and attention to nonverbal communication can reveal
the intensity of those interests. Their knowledge of other stakeholders can
reveal their ties to them and, often, the influence of other stakeholders in
the project's larger network.

As the project progresses, project leaders need to spend time working
with the more influential stakeholders and those who have access to

important project resources. These meetings can happen in formal places like project meetings or less formal places like luncheons.

Many project leaders shy away from these kinds of networking tasks. Often coming from a more technical background, they prefer to work on the project itself rather than on the networks that surround the project. Successful leaders, however, spend much of their time on such networking tasks. The social capital provided by project networks provides project leaders with the information, support, and other resources that they need to be successful. Project leaders should not think of networking work as taking them away from project work. Rather, networking *is* the kind of project work required of them.

SUMMARY

Projects never exist in isolation. They are surrounded by a network of stakeholders, often with different interests in the project, who can determine its success or failure. In this chapter, we examined various stakeholders, their interests, and how project leaders might respond to them. We went on to examine the networks to which stakeholders belong and the role of the project leader in developing and working with those networks.

Stakeholders are those who have an interest or stake in the conduct or outcomes of a project. We examined eight kinds of stakeholders in this chapter. Project clients are those who sponsor or fund a project. They are interested in the project because it is supposed to address some set of their needs. At the beginning of a project, leaders often need to help clients clarify their needs and how they might be addressed by concrete project deliverables. This is one of the most valuable services project leaders can provide to their clients as well as to the future project team. During the course of the project, clients often like to be kept informed of its progress. This is best done with structured progress reports and with additional communications as required. The transfer of final project deliverables signals the conclusion of the project. Project leaders want to meet or exceed client expectations with those deliverables and need to manage those expectations from the beginning to the end of the project. Project leaders often find checklists a useful tool to focus attention on the key deliverables of a project. Often, postdelivery work must be done to fully close the project and satisfy the client. The time and costs of postdelivery work should be incorporated into project plans.

Managers in the host organization are also important stakeholders, and one's direct supervisor is key among them. Host organization managers want the project to proceed as planned, and project leaders want managers to support and champion their projects. Providing structured progress reports to management, keeping management informed of strategic issues and problems, and handling minor problems efficiently will generally conform to management expectations.

The project team is an important stakeholder as well. The team members want to know that they can bring the project to a successful conclusion. At the beginning of a project, the team wants the leader to provide clear project objectives and action plans. The members want the leader to provide the necessary resources to do the project when they are needed and to buffer the project team from unnecessary outside pressures. Project members often have commitments other than the project itself and they would like the leader to plan for those commitments as well.

External suppliers or vendors are another class of stakeholder. They provide often critical and unique resources to the project, and the scheduled delivery of those resources according to specification is important to project success. Project leaders are well advised to check on the delivery of resources prior to their scheduled transfer and to develop deeper relationships with more critical vendors.

Internal suppliers are those in the host organization who supply the project with resources such as personnel and information. Even when the provision of resources is expected and planned, those providing resources may see their provision as an imposition. Project leaders need to be sensitive to these issues and work with the supplying unit as closely as possible. Although problems with internal supply might have to be taken to higher level management, they are best resolved at lower levels.

Regulators have a stake in the quality of the conduct or output of a project. Their aim is to certify conformance to regulatory standards. Project leaders should pay particular attention to regulatory requirements in the planning, budgeting, and execution of project work. In some cases, the use of outside experts to review the project or its output can help address certification needs.

End users and implementers are postproject stakeholders. Projects are often designed to benefit users other than the sponsoring clients themselves. Project leaders and clients should discuss the end users' needs in the planning and budgeting stages of the project. Implementers—those who will implement the project's recommendations—are also an important stakeholder to keep in mind. Although projects often implement the products and services they produce, many do not. In those cases, the more the project team knows of the challenges implementers will face, the more action-oriented and useful their recommendations can be. Materials and resources are often uncovered during the course of a project that can be useful to implementers. Simply cataloging those resources is a low-cost, value-added component project leaders should consider providing.

Finally, projects have political stakeholders. Projects are designed to change things. Changes create benefits and losses for those affected by them. Those who see a loss because of the conduct or outcome of a project can be expected to oppose it. Those who see benefits are likely to be supporters. Unfortunately, project success itself may also threaten those who see themselves in competition with the project leader for promotions and the like. It is a good idea, then, for project leaders to think through the political aspects of their projects as well as the technical ones.

Project stakeholders are tied to each other and form project networks. Being able to work well in these networks increases a project leader's social capital. Social capital comes from one's relationships with others who can provide help to a project. Although many project leaders would prefer to concentrate on the primary project team, the success of their project also rests on their ability to develop ties with the broader array of stakeholders in the project network. Many if not most of these ties are not strong. They are the weaker kind of ties expected in resource-sharing business arrangements—friendly but entirely business-related. Stronger ties should be developed by cultivating relationships with the individuals most critical to the project and to the project leader's career.

Project leaders should start developing their social capital early in the planning phase of a project by identifying stakeholders and making initial contacts. These contacts are best made face-to-face and one-on-one to facilitate better communications. As the project progresses, the leader needs to spend more time with the more influential stakeholders of the project. Although many project leaders shy away from this kind of networking, they need to understand that it is a critical part of their project leadership role.

REVIEW QUESTIONS

1. What is a project stakeholder?

2. Compare and contrast the interests of project clients and higher management in the host organization.

3. What are the similarities and differences between external and internal suppliers?

   a. How should a project leader attend to each?

4. What are the roles political stakeholders can play in a project?

   a. What are the factors that affect whether political stakeholders will emerge?

5. What is meant by social capital?

    a. What role do strong ties and weak links play in social capital?

6. Why do some project leaders have more social capital than others?

7. How does a project leader go about developing his or her social capital?

EXERCISES

1. You are a project leader of a project to increase the efficiency of loading and unloading material from your company's dock.

    a. Who are the likely stakeholders in your project?

    b. How should you address their interests?

2. You are the leader of a project to set up a new store for your company. The company wants to open up 100 of these stores nationwide in the next year. The project entails finding a suitable location in a specific geographic area designated by the company and developing a turnkey operation—one that is ready for immediate use.

    a. Who are the likely stakeholders in your project?

    b. How should you address their interests?

3. Take a quick inventory of your social capital. Do so by first identifying the strong social ties you have to others in your organization (you can use your college as an organization if you are a student). Next, identify your weak links to important and influential people in your organization. Is the profile of your social capital more like Figure 7.1, 7.2, or 7.3?

4. You have just been put in charge of an important project in your organization that will affect a number of operations directly and indirectly.

    a. Define this project in any way you wish.

    b. Discuss how you would go about developing your social capital on this project. Be as specific as you can.

ENDNOTES

1. Managers tend to have preferences about the nature or kind of reports they like (e.g., verbal or written, extensive or summary), the timing of them, and their contents (e.g., covering only problems that have arisen or furnishing more detail about current budget use, progress, and the like). It is an important aspect of project leadership, then, to know your supervisor's preferences and meet them to his or her satisfaction.

2. I recall a story about a Canadian high-rise construction firm that consistently came in on budget and on schedule in all its projects—an almost unheard-of success story. It turned out that one of its secrets was that it made sure workers got the materials they needed when they needed them. Having project resources available when project members need them is a vital part of project success.

3. Sometimes, closer working relationships develop between project leaders and some of the regulators who oversee their work. If that is the case, it is important not to abuse the relationship. Project leaders need to work with the regulator to meet the standards required, not to bypass them.

4. Many projects are designed primarily for the end user or ultimate customer. For example, new medicines are designed for the end user even though the costs of research and development are borne by the sponsoring clients. Project success depends on how the end user benefits. Project leaders, then, should keep an interest in the end user. Sponsoring clients often have their interests in mind. Clients may also rehire project teams or their host organizations to follow up on and carry out their own recommendations or some part of them for the end user. A project's clear commitment to users will increase this likelihood.

5. Kakabadse, A., & Parker, C. (Eds.). (1984). *Power, politics, and organizations: A behavioral science view*. New York, NY: John Wiley. Pfeffer, J. (1981). *Power in organizations*. Marshfield, MA: Pitman. Mintzberg, H. (1983). *Power in and around organizations*. Englewood Cliffs, NJ: Prentice Hall.

6. Ancona, D. G., & Caldwell, D. (1992). Bridging the boundary: External activity and performance in organizational teams. *Administrative Science Quarterly*, 37, 634–665. These authors also address how teams can play this same function.

7. Coleman, J. (1988). Social capital in the creation of human capital. *American Journal of Sociology*, 94, 95–120. See also Leana, C. R., & Van Buren, H. J., III. (1999). Organizational social capital and employment practices. *Academy of Management Review*, 24, 538–556.

8. Burt, R. S. (1992). *The social structure of competition*. Cambridge, MA: Harvard University Press. Burt, R. S. (1999). Entrepreneurs, distrust, and third parties: A strategic look at the dark side of defense works. In L. Thompson, J. Levine, & D. Messick (Eds.), *Shared cognition in organizations: The management of knowledge* (pp. 213–243). Mahwah, NJ: Lawrence Erlbaum. Adapted by Thompson, L. L. (2004). *Making the team: A guide for managers* (2nd ed.). Upper Saddle River, NJ: Prentice Hall.

KEY TERMS

Capital: any asset that can be employed to produce wealth.

Clients: those for whom the project is being conducted as well as the ultimate source of resources for the project.

End Users: those who will ultimately use or benefit from the project.

External Regulators: independent organizations or agencies with formal responsibility and authority to certify project work and output.

External Suppliers: those outside the organization who provide project resources.

Host Organization Management: higher level managers within the organization where the project is conducted.

Human Capital: the knowledge, skills, and abilities of a person that can be used to produce things of value, such as deliverables from project tasks.

Implementers: those who will carry out the project's recommendations.

Internal Regulators: regulators who work for the host organization and generally attend to the conduct of the project.

Internal Suppliers: those within the host organization who supply the project with resources.

Political Players: those who use their influence to either support or oppose the project based on their own interests and aims.

Project Team: the group of people who are actually carrying out project activities.

Regulators: those who make sure projects achieve established levels of quality in their conduct or output.

Scope Creep: when the scope of the project slowly begins to expand after it has begun. This often happens when clients get ideas for additional products and services they would like included in the project.

Social Capital: the value someone has because he or she can tap into various social networks to get the resources needed for a job.

Stakeholders: those people, organizational units, and institutions that have a vested interest in the project and can affect it in some way.

8

Leading Project Teams

INTRODUCTION

JOHN'S PROMOTION

John Billings was looking at his boss, Mark White, feeling a new admiration for the man, but also feeling more than nervous about what this meeting meant for him. John's boss had been promoted to department head in their division of APEX, a large government-contracting firm. When Mark received his promotion, he recommended John to fill his position: one of three section leaders who report to the department head. John jumped at the opportunity and soon would receive a hefty increase in salary along with his promotion.

In this meeting, Mark was laying out the various accounts John would be taking over when these feelings of admiration and anxiety began to emerge. Two accounts were still in the negotiation stage. One account was ready to launch. Three more were continuing projects, but one of those was scheduled for closing at the end of the month.

John knew everyone in the section, of course, but now he would be dealing with them in a whole new way as section manager. In addition, he would be dealing much more closely with higher management, clients, and others outside the department in his new position.

John admired Mark because he really was a good leader and obviously deserved his promotion. His boots would be hard to fill; and that began to make John nervous. Despite working on projects in the section for some time now, John realized that he had only the smallest notion of what he would have to do to be successful in his new role as a project manager.

CHAPTER OVERVIEW

John's concerns are widely shared by those new to leadership positions, whether they are taking over a single project or a whole "section-load" of them like John. This entire book is devoted to project leadership issues, but here we address three more sets of issues. The first concerns expectations others have of a project leader. Project leaders are called on to play many, often conflicting, roles for various stakeholders. We identify many of the more common role expectations and offer some advice about addressing them.

The second set focuses on the leadership of a project team throughout the life of a project. Project leaders need to lead projects differently depending on where they are in their life cycle. John, for example, will need to lead each of his project teams differently because the projects are at different stages in their life cycles. He will also have to work with each project's other stakeholders differently for the same reason. We examine the different needs of projects depending on their life cycle stage and what leaders should do to address those needs.

The final set of issues deals with the leadership needs of individual project members. Project personnel come and go on projects and need different kinds of leadership depending on their "job maturity" in doing the project's work. We finish this chapter by discussing individual project member leadership needs and how best to develop project staff.

THE ROLES OF A PROJECT LEADER

Leaders are expected to play a role in their organizations just like everyone else. The leadership role, however, is complex, and different people have very different, often conflicting expectations of a leader. Because the leadership role is so critical to project success, we examine some of the more typical expectations stakeholders have of a project leader. We conclude by suggesting how leaders can negotiate some of the expectations stakeholders have of them.

The roles played by organizational leaders have been studied for some time. Two particularly well-known and appropriate studies are those done by Henry Mintzberg[1] and Luthans and Lockwood.[2] Although Mintzberg focused on higher level managers and Luthans and Lockwood focused on supervisors, their studies share some common elements that are particularly applicable to project leaders. They are integrated here with an eye toward the role demands of project leaders. We classify them into those role expectations held by external and internal stakeholders.

EXTERNAL ROLE REQUIREMENTS

Figurehead and Spokesperson

By the nature of their position, project leaders are the **figureheads** of their projects. They are called on to represent their projects at most, if not all, public functions. It is important, then, for project leaders to display proper demeanor in all public venues. Stakeholder and public judgments of the project and its team are influenced a great deal by the demeanor and behavior of its chief representative.

As the chief representative of the project, leaders are also called on to be their project's **spokesperson,** whether giving formal presentations of the project before large groups or speaking one-on-one with individual stakeholders. It is important for project leaders to be up to date on the status of their projects and to be able to communicate the progress, needs, and benefits of their projects to external stakeholders when required.[3]

Liaison and Monitor

In the previous chapter, we explored the key position project leaders occupy at the center of the larger network of project stakeholders. Because of that position, most project business is conducted through project leaders in their role as **liaison** to the project.[4] Project leaders need to actively embrace, develop, and maintain their liaison role, not only for the good of their projects but for the good of their own careers as well.

The liaison role has both a formal and an informal side to it. Formally, project leaders are called on to do business with suppliers, clients, management, the public, and other stakeholders. Informally, project leaders are often expected to socialize with stakeholders to develop closer ties with them. Many project leaders are less comfortable performing this role, and socializing can be quite time-consuming. Shareholder concerns, problems, and opportunities for the project, however, are often first encountered, and can be dealt with more effectively, on these informal occasions.

The project leader also plays a role as the project's **monitor.** The project network is a principal source of information about stakeholder needs, concerns, resources, and intentions with regard to the project. In the role of monitor, the project leader needs to continually observe the network of stakeholders to get important project information, anticipate project problems, and take advantage of opportunities as they arise.

Champion and Negotiator

Project leaders are often expected to be the **champions** of the projects they lead. Project leaders must be able to communicate the benefits and needs of their projects in terms that speak to stakeholder interests. Working with their ties in the larger project network, leaders also need to help members of their project team resolve difficulties they may encounter outside the team.

Because of their position, stakeholders turn to project leaders as the **chief negotiator** for the project. The negotiation role is particularly pronounced in the early stages of a project. When stakeholders first come together, all project parameters—scope, costs, and schedule—are open for negotiation.[5] The project leader's key objective in these negotiations is to ensure project success. What "success" means for the project in terms of its objectives, and what the project requires to be successful, need to be realistically matched.

Negotiations also occur throughout the execution of the project. Stakeholders often ask for more products or for other project changes as they clarify earlier expressions of their needs. Project leaders may have to adapt to these adjustments, known as scope creep, but must work to make sure that they get the additional time and resources to do so.

Controller

Clients and higher management in the host organization expect project leaders to control their projects. Essentially, the **controller** role means that the project leader makes sure the project is proceeding as planned—producing deliverables according to specifications, in line with the budget, and on schedule. Day-to-day problems with project tasks are generally expected to be handled within the project itself. Larger problems may arise, however, to threaten the project's deliverables, costs, schedule, or other outcomes. Because projects are unique endeavors, these problems are not uncommon—the more unique and complex the project, the more common the problems. Project leaders need to monitor their projects carefully, then, to spot emerging problems early and deal with them, as covered in Chapter 5 on risk management. If problems need to be brought to the attention of stakeholders, however, project leaders should have plans about how to regain control of the project and what resources are needed to do so.

INTERNAL ROLE REQUIREMENTS

Planner and Resource Allocator

As **planner,** the project leader is expected to take the lead on all project planning. Although others may help in developing project plans, the responsibility for planning lies with the project leader. Team members look to the project leader to make sure project plans are doable. Project planning, moreover, is an ongoing process in project work. As a project unfolds, it becomes apparent that the best-laid plans have not been able to anticipate everything.

Project leaders are expected to look ahead in the project to spot and plan for unanticipated needs and changes.

Much the same can be said for what project leaders should do in their role as the **resource allocator** for the project. Initial project plans, of course, require project leaders to allocate resources among project activities. As the project moves forward, however, project leaders may need to shift resources from one activity to another, for example, to keep the project on schedule. Experienced project members know that resource reallocations are often required and that they may have to do the same or more work with less. That knowledge, however, does not completely ease their disappointment. It is important, then, that project leaders inform their teams as soon as possible when resources need to be reallocated and to tell those involved why such changes are necessary.[6]

Coordinator

As the project's **coordinator,** leaders need to ensure that all pieces of the project and the project team are working together toward their common project objectives. Although coordination is also a need in general management, when operations reach a steady state, coordination can be achieved with standard operating procedures. Despite all the efforts made in project planning, steady states are rare in project environments. Coordination, therefore, requires much more real-time work. Leaders will find that they need to meet often with their project teams and individual members to keep the project coordinated. Time needs to be set aside, then, for project meetings as part of the project plan itself (for a few tips on project meetings see the sidebar on Conducting Project Meetings).[7]

CONDUCTING PROJECT MEETINGS

An important task that usually falls to the project leader is to plan and conduct project meetings. Unfortunately, there is almost universal agreement that meetings are often poorly run, and many meetings are a waste of time. Project leaders can make meetings cost-effective if they keep a few things in mind: Meetings are like any other project task and need to be treated as such. Meetings also need to be planned and executed well and need to be properly followed up. These are covered, in turn, here.

- Meetings are like any other project task.

Project meetings are a necessary administrative support task. They need to be integrated into the work breakdown structure (WBS) and scheduled in the project. Project meetings should have their own objectives with deliverables to achieve them. Plans need to be made to produce those deliverables, including the allocation of human resources (e.g., leader, scribe, participants) and other resources.

Two basic kinds of project meetings can be planned ahead of time: those for outside stakeholders and those for the project team. Meetings for outside stakeholders (e.g., clients and higher management in the host organization) are often scheduled at specific milestones in the project with meeting objectives related to those milestones. Some outside stakeholders might also wish to have periodic, recurring meetings just to keep informed about the project.

Project team meetings are primarily of two types: meetings at specific milestones and recurring periodic meetings. Team meetings at specific milestones (e.g., project launch, closedown, preparations for outside stakeholders at their milestones) will also have their objectives and deliverables related to those milestones. Recurring team meetings (e.g., every week or two) are conducted for a variety of task objectives such as real-time coordination of the project, information sharing, decision making, monitoring the project, and problem solving, among others. Project leaders should also be aware that team meetings are a venue to address socio-emotional or group maintenance issues such as attending to team morale and cohesion; resolving conflict issues; and developing and maintaining team norms, roles, and goals. A regularly scheduled meeting need not be held if these objectives and issues do not need attention or can be achieved in a more cost-efficient way. Attention is given here primarily to recurring team meetings and the task needs of the project.

- Project meetings need to be planned

The principal planning tool of any meeting is the meeting's agenda. The agenda can be thought of as the WBS of the meeting—the meeting's breakdown of discussion topics. Just as important, the agenda is also the principal organizing tool of the meeting.

An agenda contains more than just a listing of discussion topics. The primary issues relevant to each topic are laid out as well (try to keep them few in number). The project leader is assumed to take the lead on an agenda item unless that role is assumed by another meeting participant (e.g., a team member who is addressing a problem in his or her part of the project). Any expected outcomes are also specified (e.g., a decision or some coordinated response to a problem).

Agenda items also trigger other activities. If participants need information about an upcoming topic, it is sent to them (it's best to have copies at the meeting as well). Discussion leaders are tasked with their job (often the agenda itself is enough, but they may need some additional tasking). Any equipment required is reserved.

(Continued)

(Continued)

Agendas are sent out ahead of time so that participants know what to expect and can give the topics and issues some thought and preparation before the meeting. The start and end times of the meeting are given and where it is to be held. At this time, input regarding the agenda is invited so that last-minute changes can be avoided. Participant input is evaluated in terms of the objectives of the meeting and whether it is the best venue for the participant to achieve his or her aims.

If possible, recurring team meetings should be scheduled to minimize interruption of workflow. Before regular work begins in the morning and just before lunch can be considered. Attention might lag just after lunch and at the end of the day. Consider a venue away from distractions yet convenient to get to.

Recurring team meetings are typically kept to an hour. If much more time is needed, consider another meeting or how issues might be handled outside the meeting. If much less time is needed, consider cancelling the meeting and covering the issues in another meeting or outside the meeting. Major milestone team meetings (e.g., project launch) may take a half a day or more.

- Conducting the meeting

The project leader usually conducts the meeting, but participants usually take the lead in their own presentations. A scribe is assigned to take relevant notes for later dissemination. The primary duty of the meeting leader is to keep the meeting focused on working through the items on the agenda and achieving the aims of the meeting. A balance is maintained between facilitating relevant discussion without wandering too far off topic.

Meeting norms need to be established and maintained. Meetings should start on time and end on or ahead of time. Participants need to stay focused on the task at hand—no irrelevant or disruptive side talking, texting, Internet surfing, and so forth. Interruptions should be minimized. Relevant participation should be encouraged and facilitated.

The meeting leader should open with a review of the agenda, invite comments or additions (hopefully few), and then walk through the discussion topics, ensuring input from relevant team members. When discussion of a topic is concluded, any action items are tasked out, acknowledged, and recorded by the scribe for later dissemination. Follow-up on these action items may well be added to the agendas of future meetings.

At the conclusion of the meeting, the leader summarizes the main developments important to the team, including action items and their tasking. Finally, clarifying input is requested and integrated; and the meeting is then brought to a close.

- Meeting follow-up

Minutes of the meeting should be disseminated to the participants. Nonparticipants who will be affected by the outcomes of the meeting are informed and their needs and actions coordinated in the project. Those tasked with action items are informed (the minutes may be enough) and their needs and actions coordinated with the rest of the project if needed.

Problem Solver

Because projects are unique endeavors, project leaders are generally confronted with a constant stream of problems. Although project leaders should develop and empower their teams to solve problems as they arise, the project leader has ultimate authority and responsibility for problem solving in his role as **problem solver.**

Few people like problems, and it is only natural to try to ignore or hide them. Project leaders, however, need to develop another mindset with the project team: Bring up problems before they get out of hand. With proper development and empowerment of the project team, team members will bring both problems and proposed solutions. Proposed solutions will need the consent of project leaders, however, because they are more aware of the ramifications of both the problem and the proposed solution on other components of the project.

Team Leader

Teams expect their leaders to lead them. In their role as **team leaders,** project leaders are expected to take the lead in all the major task and operational decisions of the project from project initiation to closedown. Teams also often expect their leaders to take the lead in handling the social-psychological or "people" issues that arise in every project. There are an endless number of social-psychological issues that confront project leaders, but motivation, discipline, and conflict management are three of the most common ones. Making sure to reward good work is the more pleasant side of motivating team members. Surprisingly, it is often overlooked, and the consequences of *not* rewarding good work can have quite a negative effect. Disciplining is often the more difficult side of the team leader role. The team expects project leaders, however, to spot and address lower performing members in a productive way. Here, too, there are important negative effects of *not* providing discipline when it is needed.

Conflict is also a common problem in projects because of the stresses and strains within them. Demanding schedules, unanticipated problems and the dependencies team members have with one another are only a few reasons why conflict emerges in a project. Conflicts over how best to do project tasks are not necessarily bad when they expose problems and help develop solutions. When conflict becomes more personal, however, project performance is likely to decrease. Knowing the difference and how best to manage conflict is also an important part of the team leader role.[8]

Project leaders are often so focused on task responsibilities that they can miss social-psychological problems until they grow to the point that they begin to undermine the project's performance. Leaders need to keep lines of communication open, not just on task issues but on social-psychological ones as well. Is coordination becoming difficult? Is communication within the team and with the project leader beginning to suffer? Is absenteeism on the rise? Are team members complaining about one another instead of task problems? These kinds of issues often signal people problems. As with task problems, dealing with social-psychological problems early in their development is far easier than dealing with them later.

CLARIFYING THE LEADERSHIP ROLE

It is easy to become overwhelmed with the project leader's responsibilities. Most project leaders will attest, however, that the real problem is the conflicting and widely different expectations that team members and external stakeholders have of them. The project leader's role will never be an easy one to play. Project leaders, however, can take the lead in helping to *make* their own role rather than just *take* the role expectations of others. To do this, project leaders need to discuss their role expectations with critical stakeholders (e.g., clients, managers, and team members). Project leaders, for example, should set aside time during the launch of a project to discuss their expectations of the team and to solicit and discuss the team's expectations as well. The same can be said of working with managers and clients—first probing their expectations, and then discussing what can be done to address their most important needs. Although confronting and discussing role expectations will never solve all role problems, it can go a long way toward reducing them to manageable levels.

PROJECT LEADERSHIP AND THE PROJECT'S LIFE CYCLE

Different leadership behaviors are typically needed to respond to the needs found in different stages of the project's life cycle. We begin by examining the leadership needs typically required in the early stages of initiation and planning, followed by those required in a project's launch. Next, we examine leadership needs in the execution phase from two perspectives: needs of the internal team and those of external stakeholders. Finally, we take a look at the project's closing stage, which needs to address concerns of the client, the host organization, and the project team. These stages become more apparent and distinct in longer projects. In shorter projects, they can blur into one another, but their leadership needs remain the same.

THE EARLY STAGES: INITIATION AND PLANNING

The initial stages of **project initiation and planning** begin when work first starts on a client's project. It ends when the leader finishes planning and organizing the project and is ready to launch it. Chapters 2, 3, and 4 are dedicated to the issues involved in the early planning stages of a project. We summarize and elaborate on a few of their key points here to address three leadership objectives in the early stages of project work. The first objective in this stage is to make sure the project is doable. The second is to organize the project, and the third is to begin acquiring the resources necessary to carry out the project.

There are at least two key issues leaders must address to make sure a project is doable. First, project leaders must determine the project's objectives and deliverables as well as their requirements in terms of the project's parameters—its work scope, costs, and schedule. The second part of making sure a project is doable is to develop agreement between the client, higher management in the host organization, and the project leader over these issues. That way, key stakeholders accept and support the project as planned.

Often, the most challenging of these initial tasks is to establish the project's deliverables. Clients often have only a vague idea of what they need in order to solve the problems they face. Project leaders, then, must help clients express and clarify their needs in terms of what a project can produce.

As a project's deliverables begin to be defined, the project parameters become issues as well—the work required, the costs, and the timeline. As they do, pressures begin to mount between clients, the host organization, and the project leader regarding their specifics and what is reasonable for stakeholders to expect. Project leaders need to anticipate such pressures and negotiate for the critical requirements that will make a project feasible.

Once project stakeholders have agreed to these project's components, the leader's attention turns to more detailed planning of the project. Attention turns, as well, to organizing the project. The project needs to be organized from the broader project level down to the level of individual work. At the broader project level, the project leader needs to determine the project's basic organizational structure. Here, project leaders lay out the major phases of project work as well as the project's authority structure—what positions will have responsibility and authority for accomplishing the various components of project work.[9] At the more detailed levels of the project, leaders should break down client and other project-relevant deliverables into the specific task deliverables required from each project member. The work breakdown structure and project scheduling covered in Chapters 3 and 4 are extremely useful tools in accomplishing these tasks.

Finally, the leader is called upon to set up and align project resources. The key resource in any project is the project team itself. Although some project leaders have a standing staff, many do not. In this case, as a project begins to form, leaders should start thinking about and recruiting key project personnel. The earlier this can be done, the better, for at least three reasons. First, there will be competition for good staff—recruiting them early helps to ensure their availability. Second, key staff can serve as expert advisors in the project's planning. Third, as the project moves forward, key staff involved in planning can better assist in the project's launch and execution.

The project leader needs to think about securing other project resources as well. Those resources that are critical and more difficult to obtain command a leader's greatest attention. In-house resources may fall into this category. Those who have authority over the use of these resources are rarely happy about letting others use them. The earlier leaders address problems of resource commitment, the better.

Involvement in the early stages of a project provides leaders with two important outcomes. First, they have the opportunity to shape the project in ways that are best for the project and their teams. The second is that they will develop a deeper understanding of the project, which will serve as the foundation for future project direction and control. This deep understanding eventually takes the form of the project plan. In some cases, projects are simply handed to leaders to execute, and they have little opportunity to shape them. In those cases, it is still imperative for leaders to develop a deep understanding of the project, its components, and the rationale behind them.

Project Launch

Project launch begins when the leader initiates the execution of project work with the project team. The short-term objectives are to orient the team and have it begin work on project deliverables in an organized manner. The longer term goal is for the project team to assume management of the project's work as they move into the execution stage of the project.[10]

When a project is first launched, project members generally look to their leaders to tell them about the project and what they are to do. The more leaders demonstrate knowledge of the project, its needs, and their ability to handle them, the more confidence team members will have in them.

Initially, leaders should summarize the important outcomes of the initiation and planning stages so the team can be brought up to speed. The objective is to help the project team understand the project and their roles in it. The project's mission, objectives, and client deliverables should be presented first. This establishes the basic directions and goals of the project. Next, leaders should lay out the project's work and organizational structure. This tells the team how the goals will be achieved and what role each team member will play. This is an opportune time, as well, to present the basic norms of the project. Producing quality work on schedule is an important project norm to establish. A "no-surprise" norm might be another—when team members see problems ahead, they need to let their leaders know as soon as possible.

Once the leader conveys an overall picture of the project to the team, he or she should provide more details, down to the individual member level—the specific deliverables each member is to provide and when. Deliverables due early in the project should receive greater attention. With small projects and teams, this might be done all at once with everyone present. With larger projects, this might require a series of meetings focusing on different components of the project.

During the initial launch, team members want, and leaders should generally adopt, a more directive style of leadership—where the leader tells the team what needs to be done. The leader's objectives are to inform the team about the project and their roles in it, and to get project work moving ahead. Team members generally have these same desires and expect their leaders to proceed in this manner. Although questions of clarification will help the team move forward, arguments about the rationale behind the planning and execution of the project are usually better handled one-on-one.[11]

Once the project is understood by the project team, the leader's attention should concentrate on initial project work, focusing on both task and resource needs. Task attention focuses on whether project tasks have been initiated properly. Performing new tasks, for example, requires close attention until the team moves up the learning curve. Early production problems also may require attention, so initial work can proceed more productively. This is also a time to address any issues of task commitment. Leaders should pay attention to team members' task focus and the time spent on them. Resource attention focuses on making sure resources are flowing as they should—that the tools, material, staff, information, and other resources are available when needed. Then, as the team settles into its work, the project moves into its execution stage.

PROJECT EXECUTION

Project execution begins when project work has been fully delegated to the project team, and project members have settled into producing the project's deliverables. It ends when the project enters its final, closing stage. The objective is to keep the project on track, and the project plan is the project leader's principal tool with its list of deliverables, work breakdown structure, schedule, and budget. To keep the project on track, leaders must accomplish a number of tasks during the execution phase of a project. Our focus is on monitoring and controlling project work in the project team and tracking the more critical external stakeholders: the client, higher management, resource suppliers, and regulators. Our discussions also focus more on the behavioral side of project leadership than on the technical issues of project control.

The Project Team

There is an old management saying: "You need to inspect what you expect." Leaders need to monitor project work to make sure it is progressing as needed. Different leaders monitor their projects and supervise their teams differently, but this may be more a matter of leadership style than leadership principles.[12] Too-close supervision can get in the way of good performance and staff development. Too little supervision can let the project get so far off track that it is difficult, if not impossible, to complete it on time or on budget.

As a rule, project leaders should not wait too long to see concrete, measurable progress being made on a project task, component, or phase. People have a natural tendency to put off work until near its delivery time in order to deal with other pressing matters. Sometimes staff may wrestle with project problems until too much time has passed before seeking help. When project staff must produce a concrete product on the way to larger project deliverables, however, it becomes much more difficult to put things off for too long. If, for example, a project job requires the results of a particular study, the design of the study, the acquisition of study resources, data gathering, analysis, and the writing of the final report are all subtasks that must be done to produce the study. The results of each subtask, then, can become a concrete deliverable that can be reviewed on the way to the ultimate product of the study itself. This kind of work breakdown is best done in the earlier stages of planning and conveyed to the project team as part of the project package in the project's launch.[13]

Project monitoring involves comparing what has been accomplished to what should have been accomplished by a certain time, and the project plan is the leader's principal tool. On many smaller, less complex projects, monitoring project deliverables is enough—comparing what has been produced to what should have been produced according to the schedule.

Cost analysis becomes more important on more complex projects as well as those done for profit. One way to monitor costs is to simply compare the actual costs of project work completed to what was budgeted for the work. When actual costs exceed budgeted costs, there is cause for concern—the more so the greater the difference.

Both costs and progress can be monitored using earned value analysis. The budgeted cost of work actually performed is a cost measure of how far along project work has progressed. At any particular date on the schedule, this figure can be compared to scheduled costs (i.e., the budgeted costs of work scheduled to be done by that date). This comparison will show, in dollar terms, how much *actual* project work is ahead or behind *scheduled* work. Although earned value analysis focuses only on the cost dimension of projects, it is a common method used to monitor complex projects. Cost deviations in actual versus budgeted costs or budgeted costs and scheduled costs serve as triggers for deeper investigations. The particulars of earned value analysis are beyond the scope of this chapter, but they are presented in more detail in Appendix B.

When project progress begins to slip, leaders need to consider at least four potential causes: project problems, deliverable problems, logistical problems, and staffing problems. **Project problems** generally reside in the project's organizational structure. One common problem is that the work breakdown structure failed to lay out the project's true work scope—the work that needed to be done. Another common project problem is poor scheduling of project staff.

Deliverable problems arise from the work on producing deliverables. Technical problems, for example, may take longer to solve than anticipated. Another example might be problems working with external stakeholders (e.g., auditees resisting audits or trainees not acquiring skills as quickly as anticipated).[14] **Logistical problems** occur when required resources are not getting to the right locations when needed (e.g., equipment, materials, or information).

Staffing problems are often problems of ability or commitment. Problems of ability lie in the required knowledge, skills, and abilities to do project work (e.g., lack of experience or adequate training). Problems of commitment are seen in terms of effort and time on task. Commitment problems can come from competing demands made on staff time, issues of morale, or simply the personal choice of staff members not to participate at needed levels of performance.

When diagnosing the causes of project problems, leaders need to be aware of at least two common sources of error. The first is called **egocentric bias**. People generally attribute success to their own efforts and failure or problems to forces outside themselves. Leaders can encounter this bias when working with others to find the causes of project problems. The second source of error is **internal attribution bias**. Supervisors tend to attribute the source of performance problems internally to workers—to their abilities or their commitment—rather than to external factors beyond the workers' control (e.g., the flow of resources needed to do the work). Quite often, the real source of problems lies outside the immediate control of individual workers.

The focus of concern for the project leader, of course, is getting the project back on schedule. Immediate shifting of resources may be necessary, including personnel shifts and other resource reallocations. Once the project is back on track, however, the leader should carefully consider the true causes of the problem or the same kind of problem may arise again and again.

External Stakeholders

Project success greatly depends on how well project leaders deal with external stakeholders.[15] Here, we focus on four stakeholders who are particularly important to the execution stage of the project: clients, higher management, resource suppliers, and regulators.

Clients generally want to see the project proceed as planned. The extent to which they require communications varies. Some clients require quite frequent updating; others simply wait for the project's deliverables. Most clients, however, want at least some progress reports at critical junctures or milestones of the project.

Sometimes clients will want additional work to be done as they see new opportunities emerge in the project. Leaders need to be clear about the additional costs such work will require. Other times, projects encounter problems, and clients must be approached for additional resources or time. Project leaders need to anticipate the risks of these kinds of problems in the early planning stages of a project and clearly communicate those risks to clients. When problems do emerge, leaders need to give their clients as much advance notice as possible and convey concrete plans to minimize the adverse effects of those problems.

Managers in the host organization also want to see the project proceed as planned. At times, higher management may wish to move resources from a leader's project to use in other projects. Project leaders need to explain how this will affect the project so that management can get a clear idea of the ramifications of its actions. Through all such negotiations with both clients and higher management, however, project leaders need to remember that keeping a good working relationship with them not only helps the project to move ahead but helps to retain support for the project as well.[16]

Projects often depend on getting resources from external suppliers and passing certain requirements by external regulators. Project leaders need to check with suppliers about the resources required before they are actually needed. The amount of lead time needed depends on how well each supplier has delivered in the past. New suppliers of critical resources should be carefully tracked. Required regulatory reviews also need close attention and careful preparation because certification is often critical to project progress. Remember, both suppliers and regulators are pulled in many different directions by demands of their own, and any particular project can drop from their attention. Project leaders should make sure that these external stakeholders are aware of the project schedule and its importance for project completion.

PROJECT CLOSING

The **project closing** phase begins when the project begins with final project delivery and ends with a project review by the project leader working with a few critical stakeholders. The objectives are to close the project to the satisfaction of all critical stakeholders and to learn the important lessons the project has taught the project team.

The final phase of a project is typically hectic as the project staff hurry to complete final contract requirements. During this period, it is easy to forget important details and activities that are not directly and substantively related to the main project deliverables. When working with clients, a simple checklist is a very nice tool to make sure all the bases are covered in a project's closedown.[17] As the project nears the end of the execution phase, all project leads should produce checklists for their own areas as well. The entire staff should participate with the construction of these checklists to minimize the risk of things being forgotten. One area requiring particular attention—simply because it is so often overlooked—is the administrative side of the project. Reports often need to be produced, presentations given, payroll and budgets finalized for the host organization, signatures attained, and the like. Meeting with clients personally should be high on a project leader's list, to make sure that they are satisfied with the project's deliverables.

The final act of closing a project is an after-action review, completed when the project has effectively closed down. In the military, **after-action reviews** and reports are a principal means for institutional learning—to make sure the lessons learned from the action can be applied in the future. Project leaders need to review the project once it has closed down to make sure they, too, have learned the lessons taught by the project.[18] When deciding who will participate in such a review, project leaders should make sure that the exercise remains a constructive one, not an opportunity to vent about problems. Leaders should choose participants who can offer candor, insight, and a wide range of perspectives but who are also committed to learning, not advancing other agendas.

After-action reviews can cover a wide range of topics. Broadly considering what was both successful and in need of future change can be a good start. Focusing on specific aspects of the project, including administrative and managerial issues as well as the technical work, can help confront issues normally overlooked. Reviewing how well different staff performed in the project can help leaders in their future recruiting. Also, reviewing relationships with important stakeholders—where things went well and where improvements might be made—can help attend to any leftover tensions as well as help leaders deal with them more effectively in the future.

PROJECT LEADERSHIP AND INDIVIDUAL PROJECT MEMBERS

One common characteristic of project work is that personnel often come and go throughout the project as needed. Some staff, of course, may come with the project's launch and leave only at the project's close. Others, however, are often needed for shorter periods during one project phase or another.

When project personnel first come on board a project, they embark on a job cycle of their own. Initially, they know relatively little about the project and what will be required of them. At these times, they tend to require a fair amount of leadership attention. Later, as they mature in their jobs, less attention is usually required.

Hersey, Blanchard, and Johnson's **Situational Leadership theory** offers project leaders some good ideas and practical advice about how to best lead individuals through this job cycle.[19] Their model is a stage model of leadership suggesting that project members mature in their jobs through four basic stages of development and that different kinds of leadership are needed at each stage. All new project members go through all stages development according to Hersey et al., but some, depending on their prior experience, develop through the stages more quickly.

The first stage of development is when members first join a project team. Hersey et al.[20] suggest that whenever someone new joins a project team, he or she needs to be led with a more directive style of leadership. **Directive leadership** is characterized more by one-way communication from the leader to the team member. The goal of directive leadership when someone first joins the project team is to orient the new person to his or her role and getting performance up to speed as quickly as possible. It is also aimed at establishing the leader's authority—that he or she is in charge of the project. New project members tend to need this kind of direction, especially from a task point of view, but they tend to want it from a people point of view as well. Most new project members want to know what is required of them and to begin their work as soon as possible.

As people settle into their project jobs and become more productive, leaders are advised to discuss with them the rationale behind their jobs and the larger project picture within which their jobs fit—a kind of "**selling leadership**" behavior. This helps them mature more in their jobs by becoming more aware of how the project as a whole is organized and the role their work and the work of others play in it. This information empowers them with the knowledge to make more important project-related decisions.

The next shift in leadership is to allow workers who are more willing and able to accept job responsibilities to participate more in the project's decision making—**participative leadership**. As problems arise and choices need to be made, participation gives project personnel "on-the-job training" in how to make good job-related judgments and decisions.

Finally, the leader is advised to delegate project work entirely to those who demonstrate the ability and willingness to take it on—**delegative leadership**. Although leaders will certainly keep tabs on things, delegation shares the leadership function with those team members who are able to assume those responsibilities. This also allows project leaders to attend to the many other tasks that confront them.

It is easy to see the parallel between Hersey et al.'s[21] leadership model and our previous recommendations about project leadership and the project's life cycle. Similar parallels can be seen with the stages of team development covered in Chapter 6. Across all these discussions, different kinds of behaviors are suggested to help leaders attend to the constantly changing needs of the project, the project team, and its members.

SUMMARY

Although project leadership entails many demands, we focused on three clusters of them. The first was the roles leaders are expected to play in their position as project leader. The second was the different kinds of leadership needed during the various stages of a project. The third was how best to lead individual project staff as they come and go on a project.

Project leaders are expected to play many roles external to their projects. Two are the roles of figurehead and spokesperson. As the figurehead, project leaders are expected to represent the project in all appropriate public functions, and they should be aware that their behavior and demeanor will reflect on their projects. As the project's figurehead, leaders are also expected to be the spokesperson for their projects. How well they present their projects to others will affect how well stakeholders think about their project and how well they think the project is being led. Project leaders also play liaison and monitor roles for their projects. Most formal business and informal contacts with the project are conducted through project leaders in their liaison role. Because project leaders are so involved with external stakeholders, they are uniquely positioned to monitor the project's environment to keep abreast of relevant project information. Project leaders are also expected to champion their projects to stakeholders in ways that get their projects the resources and support they need. Because of their positions, project leaders also generally play a key negotiating role, usually between clients, higher management, and the project team. Finally, clients and higher management expect project leaders to play a controller role for their projects. They are expected to keep the project moving forward as planned—staying on budget and on schedule. Leaders should handle the more routine problems in the context of the project. Larger problems should be brought to the attention of the appropriate stakeholder with plans for overcoming them.

Project leaders are also expected to play a variety of internal leadership roles for their project team. In their planning role, leaders are expected to take the lead on all project planning during the early stages of a project and whenever new plans are needed to adjust for project changes. Project leaders are also the key resource allocators for their projects, not only in project planning but in project execution as well. Project resources often have to be reallocated during a project, and the leader must take the lead in deciding those reallocations. Project leaders are also expected to coordinate project work and help solve problems. Coordination is an ongoing challenge in project work because a steady state is rarely achieved for long. Project leaders are also expected to take the lead in problem solving. Because projects are, by definition, unique endeavors, problems are expected. Technical and operational problems go with the territory, and project leaders need to empower their teams to solve them. The solution of technical problems may well lie outside the leader's area of expertise. Even so, all solutions that will affect the larger project need to be authorized by the leader. Finally, project leaders also play a team leader role, which has both a task component and a social-psychological component.

By definition, roles are the expectations that others have of a role holder. Those expectations can vary across those who have them and, in the case of project leaders in particular, are often in conflict. Project leaders also have their preferences for how they would like to fill these expectations. It is important, then, for leaders to negotiate and clarify the role expectations stakeholders have of them.

All these project leadership requirements change depending on the stage of a project's life cycle. Leader involvement in the early initiation and planning stages of a project is important for at least two reasons: to help shape the project and to develop a deep understanding of it for future direction and control. The leader's first responsibility is to clarify the objectives and deliverables of a project. The next obligation is to make sure the project is doable—that the work scope, costs, and time allocations are realistic. These project parameters are best established by leaders in their role as project negotiators. Once a project's parameters are established, leaders turn to organizing their projects. The principal tools for organizing are the work breakdown structure and the project's schedule. Finally, the project leader needs to acquire and align project resources. The most important resource is the project team itself. The earlier leaders can begin assembling the key members of the project team, the better. Team members can assist in planning and, as a consequence, participate more fully in the project's launch. Earlier recruitment also increases the probability of getting qualified key personnel.

The project's launch is a particularly critical event in its life cycle. The short-term objective is to make sure project work is properly begun. The longer term objective is to lay the foundation so that project work can eventually be delegated to the project team during the project's execution phase. Leaders need to demonstrate their knowledge and command of the project during this critical period, and project teams expect them to do so. Summarizing the important objectives of the project, how they will be achieved, and who on the team is responsible for what aspects of the project can help achieve these objectives. Once work has begun on project tasks, leaders need to pay attention to both task and resource needs. Task attention focuses on whether project tasks have been initiated properly. Resource attention focuses on making sure resources are flowing as they should.

The primary leadership objective of project execution is to keep the project on track. First, leaders need to monitor the work of the project team. This should be done in a way that is neither too close—hurting good performance—nor too loose—letting the project go off track before taking corrective action. Receiving concrete deliverables before too much time has passed in a project is a good method for keeping the project on track. Breaking down larger deliverables with longer delivery times into smaller, interim deliverables is one useful way of accomplishing this. Leaders monitor their projects by comparing what should have been accomplished to what actually has been. The project plan with its work breakdown structure, schedule, and project budget are all used as standards for comparison. Smaller projects might focus simply on deliverables—have they been produced on schedule and according to expectations? Larger projects usually need to monitor costs more carefully by comparing, for example, budgeted costs to actual costs of project work. Earned value analysis includes the time dimension by adding scheduled costs as a standard for assessment.

During the execution phase, leaders need to keep an eye out for any problems that might be emerging from within the project team. Leaders can look to four common sources of these internal project problems: project, deliverable, logistical, and staffing problems. An example of a project problem is that the work breakdown structure did not include required work. Deliverable problems emerge from the work itself, such as having to overcome technical difficulties. Logistical problems are generally tied to the lack of resources when they are needed. Staffing problems are principally problems of ability or commitment. Either the staff do not have the ability to perform the task given to them, or they lack the commitment to do so. Although the leader needs to get the project back on track as soon as possible, searching for the real cause of project problems will help keep them from emerging in the future.

Project leaders also need to track external stakeholders during the execution phase—success depends a great deal on them. Clients want to see the project proceed as planned and sometimes want additional work to be done. Higher management also wants to see the project proceed as planned and sometimes wishes to reallocate resources to other projects. When large problems emerge to threaten the project, leaders need to inform their clients and higher management of the problems and provide plans to resolve them. When clients or management want additional work or the reallocation of resources, leaders need to make very clear how these decisions will affect the project. Because projects depend on outside suppliers and regulators, leaders also need to make sure these stakeholders are well integrated into project plans as required.

When projects close, leaders need to make sure that all the products, services, and other outcomes of a project are delivered to the client. Checklists are good tools to use in this regard. Checklists are also useful for making sure all requirements have been met with the host organization to close down the project. Finally, leaders should conduct after-action reviews to look back over the project to learn how to perform better in the future.

Just as the leadership needs for the project as a whole change as it goes through its life cycle, the leadership needs of project personnel change as well. At first, personnel need and generally want a more directive style of leadership to orient them to their job and to get them up to speed on project work. As they demonstrate their abilities to handle their jobs, the leader should spend more time letting them know how their work fits into the overall project and how the project as a whole is organized and led, using a more "selling" leadership style. This empowers the project member with the knowledge and information needed to begin making his or her own more important job-related decisions. Leadership should then shift to a more participatory style to further advance the member's job maturity in terms of being able to develop good project judgments and make good decisions about broader project issues. Finally, leaders should shift to delegating more responsibility to team members who show the ability and willingness to accept leadership responsibilities. At that point, leaders can turn their attention to other project tasks.

REVIEW QUESTIONS

1. Define and identify the expectations of the following roles of a project leader:

   a. Liaison and monitor

   b. Champion

   c. Controller

   d. Planner and resource allocator

   e. Team leader

2. Why should a project leader clarify his or her leadership role?

   a. How should he or she go about doing so?

3. Discuss the various leadership requirements in the following stages of the project's life cycle:

   a. Initiation and planning

   b. Project launch

   c. Project execution

   d. Project closing

EXERCISES

1. Review the various roles project leaders are called on to play.

   a. Assess your strengths and weaknesses for each of them.

   b. For those roles in which you are not strong, how would you address them in any given project?

2. Identify a project of your own choosing.

   a. Lay out a plan for its initiation and planning.

3. Recall a school or work project that you have recently completed.

   a. Conduct an after-action review of the project.

   b. How would you do things differently if you were the project leader (again)? In addressing this question, review and comment on what occurred in the project as it moved through its various project stages.

ENDNOTES

1. Mintzberg, H. (1973). *The nature of managerial work.* New York, NY: Harper & Row.

2. Luthans, F., & Lockwood, D. L. (1984). Toward an observation system for measuring leader behavior in natural settings. In J. G. Hunt, D. Hosking, C. A. Schriesheim, & R. Stewart (Eds.), *Leaders and managers: International perspectives on managerial behavior and leadership* (pp. 117–141). New York, NY: Pergamon.

3. It is also important for external stakeholders to get a consistent message about the project. For this reason, external communications are often restricted to the project leader. If other project members are required to interact with external stakeholders, it is important that the project leader be present if possible or thoroughly debriefed if not.

4. Often, team members will work with external stakeholders as well. It is important in these interactions that the project leader is kept thoroughly informed of important project business.

5. An excellent source for negotiation is: Fisher, R., Ury, W., & Patton, B. (1991). *Getting to yes: Negotiating agreement without giving in.* New York, NY: Penguin Books.

6. The explanations leaders give followers for their decisions have been well researched in the organizational justice literature. Laying out the causes that required the change and the project goals that will be addressed by the change can help dampen the disappointment and anger team members may have about the change. It may be that such accounts cannot be given immediately, but leaders should remember to give them as soon as possible.

7. Meetings, of course, are legitimate project activities to the extent they add value to the project over and above the costs of those who must attend them. Project leaders are expected to weigh those costs and benefits carefully.

8. For further discussion, see Jehn, K. A., & Bendersky, C. (2003). Intragroup conflict in organizations: A contingency perspective on the conflict-outcome relationship. In R. M. Kramer & B. M. Staw (Eds.), *Research in organizational behavior* (Vol. 25, pp. 187–242). Kindlington, UK: Elsevier Ltd.

9. There is an old management dictum that when more than one person has responsibility for a task, no one has responsibility for it. Although project work often requires the efforts of many, one person needs to be accountable for getting the task done.

10. The working assumption here is that a project's launch occurs with the entire team all at once. In many projects, team members join the project in different phases. The project needs to be launched to newcomers as they arrive—providing them the information they need and making sure initial work is proceeding as planned.

11. Quite often, concerns of project members are not raised in this early stage of project work. As the team moves into its storming stage, however, more concerns and disagreements about the rationale behind project issues may arise (see Chapter 6). Project leaders should not necessarily take this as insubordination but as legitimate participation over valid concerns that need to be addressed. This is often best done one-on-one.

12. Fiedler, F. E. (1967). *A theory of leadership effectiveness.* New York, NY: McGraw-Hill.

13. One rule of thumb might be the "80-hour" rule: no more than 80 hours of work (2 weeks) should pass before something concrete is delivered from a task package.

14. These kinds of problems need to be anticipated as sources of project risk early in planning and clearly communicated to clients and higher management. For more on this and other potential project problems, see Chapter 5 on the management of project risk.

15. Ancona, D. G., & Caldwell, D. (1992). Bridging the boundary: External activity and performance in organizational teams. *Administrative Science Quarterly, 37,* 634–665.

16. An excellent source for client and higher-management negotiations is Fisher et al. (1991).

17. Building contractors often use a punch list to finish off their projects. They get together with their clients to review the property and, together, negotiate a list of final things that need to be done to finish the job. The company of a project manager I know does something similar. Managers do a computer word search for all elements of their contracts that have the phrases "The company will" or "The company shall...." These phrases were placed in the contract specifying deliverables, and the word search constructs a check-off list for them.

18. As mentioned previously, lessons are really learned throughout the project and should be used as they are acquired. After-action reviews, however, offer the opportunity to wrap them up given the full advantages of hindsight.

19. Hersey, P., Blanchard, K. H., & Johnson, D. E. (1996). *Management of organization behavior: Utilizing human resources* (7th ed.). Englewood Cliffs, NJ: Prentice Hall. Their ideas are abstracted here and adjusted for project leadership needs.

20. Hersey et al. (1996).

21. Hersey et al. (1996).

KEY TERMS

After-Action Review: a report used principally for institutional learning, to make sure the lessons learned from the project can be applied in the future.

Champion: the role project leaders play when they promote the benefits and needs of their projects in terms that speak to stakeholder interests.

Chief Negotiator: the role project leaders play when they negotiate what a project is to produce and the resources required to produce it.

Controller: the role project leaders play when they make sure the project is proceeding as planned—producing deliverables according to specifications, on budget, and on schedule.

Coordinator: the role project leaders play when they ensure that the project team is working together toward common project objectives.

Delegative Leadership: leadership behavior characterized by delegating the project job to the team member entirely—although periodic checks on performance are made. This leadership style is appropriate for those workers who can handle delegation in terms of their ability and willingness to do the job on their own. The goal is to share the leadership function with those who are able to assume those responsibilities.

Deliverable Problems: problems that arise from the work in producing deliverables.

Directive Leadership: leadership behavior characterized by one-way communication from the leader to the team member. A leadership style used for new project members. The goal is to orient the new member to the job and get him or her up to speed as quickly as possible.

Egocentric Bias: the tendency for people to attribute success to their own efforts and failure or problems to forces outside themselves.

Figurehead: the role project leaders play when they represent their projects at public functions.

Internal Attribution Bias: the tendency for supervisors to attribute the source of performance problems internally to workers—to their abilities or their commitment—rather than to external factors beyond the worker's control.

Liaison: the role project leaders play when they are called on to do business with, and develop informal ties to, stakeholders.

Logistical Problems: problems in getting required resources to the right locations when needed.

Monitor: the role project leaders play when they monitor the project environment for information important to the project.

Participative Leadership: leadership behavior characterized by allowing a team member to participate in the decision-making requirements of the project that would concern him or her. This leadership style is appropriate for those team members who are more willing and able to accept responsibility for their jobs. The aim is to provide a kind of "on-the-job training" on how to make good judgments and decisions.

Personnel Problems: problems of ability or commitment among project staff.

Planner: the role project leaders play when they take the lead in all project planning.

Problem Solver: the role project leaders play as the person ultimately responsible for solving project problems.

Project Closing: the stage of the project that begins with final delivery and ends with a project review.

Project Execution: the stage of the project when project work has been fully delegated to the project team, and project members have settled into producing the project's deliverables. It ends at project closing.

Project Initiation and Planning: the stage of the project from when work first begins on the client's project to when the leader finishes planning and organizing the project.

Project Launch: the stage of the project when the leader initiates the execution of project work with the project team.

Project Monitoring: the practice of comparing what has been accomplished to what should have been accomplished by a certain time.

Project Problems: problems that come from the project itself. Often these problems are in the project's organizational structure.

Resource Allocator: the role project leaders play when they address the distribution of resources in project planning and execution.

Selling Leadership: leadership behavior characterized by more open communication between the leader and the team member. A leadership style used after project members have developed the ability to do their jobs as assigned. The goal is to help the project member develop by explaining the rationale behind why the project job is structured the way it is.

Situational Leadership Theory: Hersey, Blanchard, and Johnson's stage model of leadership suggesting that project members mature in their jobs through various stages and that different kinds of leadership are needed at each stage.

Spokesperson: the role project leaders play when they act as the primary representative of the project, such as giving formal presentations to important stakeholder groups and individuals.

Team Leader: the role project leaders play when they take the lead in all the major task decisions of the project as well as the social-psychological ones such as motivation, discipline, and conflict resolution.

9

Writing Project Reports

INTRODUCTION

THE CHINA REPORT

Tim Conway and Jennifer Lau had just finished a very tough project for their company, Tech Machine Tools. Tech Machine manufactures high-end precision tool and dye machines used by other companies to produce a wide variety of precision products. Based in Wisconsin, Tech Machines wanted to explore the feasibility of two business ventures. The first was to develop and run another manufacturing facility in southern China. The "economics" seemed attractive to Tech Machine's executives, but they needed an in-depth study of the idea. The second venture was to explore what it would take to break into the market for high-end machine tools in southern China. China's economy was growing at a very promising rate and Tech Machines would like to "get in on the action" as Dave Reynolds, the CEO, put it. The idea was to gain a foothold somewhere in that region and use it to expand to other areas of China.

Tech Machines funded this feasibility study very well and gave Tim and Jennifer—two of their rising stars—6 months to complete it. Tim took the lead on the manufacturing side of the project, and Jennifer took the lead on the marketing side. Throughout the project, organizational personnel contributed time and effort as needed; and several consultants were retained and used both in the United States and on one trip to China, where Tim and Jennifer looked closely at physical facilities, supply chains, evaluated human resources that could be tapped, and met with potential venture partners.

Now, 5 months later, Tim and Jennifer were having a cup of coffee together to celebrate almost completing the project when their conversation turned to their last project task—producing a project report. As they discussed this last task, it began to dawn on them how important yet difficult the task was. It was important because information in the report itself would be used as the basis for Tech Machine executives' deciding whether to go ahead and invest millions of dollars and perhaps years of effort into a major strategic move—one that would greatly help or hurt the company. The report would be important, too, if the decision was made to move ahead. Those who would be charged with carrying out the venture would look to the report for guidance and the information they would need to make the right decisions. It was also important to Tim and Jennifer because how well they had done the project would be judged to a great extent on how well the report itself was received. If these issues were not daunting enough, Tim and Jennifer realized that neither of them had ever written such a report before, and they were unsure how to start.

CHAPTER OVERVIEW

Project reports can differ a great deal from one another in a number of ways. They differ in their purpose, their formats, and their formality, to name just a few. They include final reports that present the project after completion, progress reports that review how a current project is progressing, and project proposals that seek to get a project funded. Even an extended e-mail to a project leader, presenting a problem that has come up and what might be done about it, could be considered a project report of sorts. Although these reports obviously differ in many ways, they have many things in common. In this chapter, we will focus on the kind of project report facing Tim and Jennifer—a formal report with all the "bells and whistles." Final reports are the focus here because many of the issues involved in their development, as well as their actual content, are relevant to other types of reports as well. Like all reports, the final report is an important deliverable designed to be used in certain ways. Its purpose is not simply to present what the project found. Like many other reports, it needs to present the information necessary to help decision makers make the decisions they face. In the case of the China Report, it is whether to invest a great deal of time, money, and resources into opening up operations in a foreign country. Still another important use of the China Report is to serve as an initial source of information to help those who will actually embark on that venture if the decision is made to move forward.

There is a wide variety of people who might read a project report, but most of the time they fall into three basic categories: decision makers, their advisors, and those who might use the report to help implement its recommendations. We begin this chapter by focusing on what each type of reader wants from a project report.

Formal reports like the one facing Tim and Jennifer can seem daunting at first. Formal reports, however, have at least one saving grace: They all have more or less the same structure. They have a "front end" with various kinds of material, a main body, and a "back end" with supporting appendices. The rest of this chapter will be devoted to working our way through these components and discussing what belongs in each of them.

KNOW YOUR READERS AND WHAT THEY WANT

Writing specialists, authors, and readers alike make one recommendation to report writers above all others: Know your readers—know what they want and how they want it delivered. Endless reports have been tossed aside because this simple recommendation was not followed. Although the advice is sound, its implementation is often difficult. When we write project reports, we tend to address our own views of the project and what we consider most important.

Generally speaking, the readers of a project report are some of the same stakeholders who have had an interest in the project all along. The time to get to know your readers, then, is not at the end of the project but from its very beginning. Project leaders need to communicate with their stakeholders all the way through a project. In their conversations, interim reports, and presentations, project leaders need to consider what stakeholders consider most important and how they want information presented to them.

We have discussed stakeholders before in terms of the roles they play: client, host manager, team members, and the like. Report readers also step into roles, and the roles they play largely determine what they are looking for in a project report and how they want it delivered. One of the most important roles is the decision maker. Decision makers will look to your report to help them make the decisions they are faced with in the future. A related role is the advisor. Advisors are often experts who help decision makers assess the quality of a report, its information, and its findings and recommendations. Still a third role is played by users or implementers of the report. Implementers look to the report to help them with the tasks they face when moving forward with report recommendations. Of course, the same reader may play all these roles, but we will examine what each wants from a report separately. We begin, however, by discussing what any reader wants from a report.[1]

What Any Reader Wants

Most readers of a project report have some general things they would like writers to keep in mind.

- *Readers want things simple.* They do not have the time or inclination to work at understanding what you are trying to say. Keep sentences simple and vocabulary straightforward; avoid jargon and acronyms that are not familiar to your readers. Keeping things simple, however, does not mean ignoring important elements and details needed by the reader.
- *Readers want what they want.* They want to jump to things that are of interest and importance to them. You need to make sure you cover what is important to your key readership and help them find it in your report.
- *Readers want what they want quickly.* They want to dig into or skim the material as they see fit. The best-written reports facilitate a quick reading of key ideas and components. Additional important detail is made quickly available to those who want it. Layout, table of contents, graphics, and the use of bullets and headings go a long way toward achieving these ends.
- *You want your readers to have confidence in your abilities.* Developing your relationship with key stakeholders during the course of the project is the best way to build stakeholder trust. How well the report is written, however, is a key element in maintaining that confidence. Poor reports can undermine even the best projects, and difficult projects can often benefit from well-prepared reports.

WHAT DECISION MAKERS WANT

One of your most important readers is the decision maker. **Decision makers** are those who have the authority to allocate resources to the project and to follow up on any recommendations the report will make. Like any other category of reader, decision makers come in all shapes and sizes. There are at least two common characteristics among them, however, that the writer should keep in mind. First, decision makers are busy people. Although your project may be first and foremost in your mind, it is likely only one of many and varied projects and tasks confronting the decision maker. Second, decision makers are paid to make things happen. As a result, they must translate the information provided in reports into concrete courses of action. Authors succeed with decision makers to the extent they help them do this. As a direct result of these two basic characteristics, formal project reports should attend to a number of issues.

- *Give background information quickly.* Because the decision maker is confronted with many tasks and projects, you will want to remind him or her quickly about your project. The **background information** needed generally includes the problem the project is addressing and the basic objectives of the project. Presenting the project's mission statement and project objectives will usually be enough. The basic activities of the project might also be included in your review of background information if you think it is required. This information is usually given in the first paragraph of an executive summary and the introduction of a formal report.

- *Think and write strategically.* When developing formal reports for decision makers, focus on key strategic issues and information relevant to them. Identify the important decisions facing decision makers and what information they need to make them.

- *Layer information according to detail.* Generally speaking, decision makers do not like to be hit with a lot of detail all at once. They like summaries first and progressively more detail as they need it while moving ahead in their decision-making process. This works out well in formal reports because different parts of the report are made for different levels of detail. The executive summary has the least amount of detail. The body of the report has more detail but still basically summarizes and explains the findings of a project. The appendices provide the most amount of detail. Separating out what is detail from what is absolutely necessary is often a difficult task for technical experts in an area. Project leaders need to keep in close contact with their readers, then, to make sure the report provides the level of detail desired.[2]

- *Avoid technical jargon.* Common phrases and vocabulary for a technical expert can be so much incomprehensible jargon to those outside the technical or specialist area. Write using the language and phrasing common to the reader, not to you.

- *Write for their level of expertise.* The expertise of decision makers is often different from that of the project writer. Fully explain ideas that may lie outside their area of expertise but don't get bogged down in unnecessary detail. Remember that decision makers are usually pretty smart, so write professionally and respectfully.

WHAT EXPERT ADVISORS WANT

Decision makers often make use of **expert advisors** to review and confirm the quality of a project report's content. Whoever plays the role of expert advisor will likely have expectations of his or her own.

Expert advisors often want to have available to them the technical detail behind the report. They expect thorough explanations that are to the point. They may also like to have available the data used in developing the project's product. Quite often, they will examine the references used in the report to make sure the project personnel are up to date and knowledgeable in the areas covered by the project.

Most of the needs expert advisors have for detail are satisfied with the use of supportive appendices. Technical issues covered and summarized in the body of the report should refer to supporting detail in an appropriate appendix. As with all readers, expert advisors want ease of access to supportive detail for their review. As the expert advisor reads through the body of the report, provide him or her with the title and page number of the supportive appendix so he or she can easily flip to the material as desired.[3]

WHAT IMPLEMENTERS WANT

Many projects are done as a first step where follow-up work is envisioned. Tim and Jennifer's feasibility study is just one example. If Tech Machine executives decide to go ahead with the venture, those who will implement the effort will turn to Tim and Jennifer's report for help. **Implementers** will use the information within the report to help carry out some or all of its recommendations or other actions decision makers have chosen to pursue. The project report, then, provides implementers with useful, and often necessary, information for their assigned task. For example, the project report developed for Linda Swain's Compliance Project in Chapter 3 would likely be used by implementers. She developed standard operating procedures for state inspections, and those procedures would likely be contained in the appendices of the final report. John's project to open the Baltimore store for Acme Auto in Chapter 2 may also be used by others even if there was no project objective to do so. If the project were deemed a success, a requested follow-up final report might be reviewed in terms of a "best practices" model for store openings.

Clearly, to the extent that implementers may need information from the report, the project leader needs to think of them as important project stakeholders. Sometimes their needs may be modest. In John's Baltimore Project write-up, a few tables and a flow chart of opening tasks may be enough. Sometimes their needs can be met with a little more work. In Linda's case, stand-alone manuals to prepare for state inspections might be needed. In Tim and Jennifer's case, however, implementers would require a great deal of information. The extent to which the project would be dedicated to addressing those needs should be assessed by project leaders at the beginning of a project and included in all project planning.[4]

THE PROJECT REPORT

Formal project reports tend to have a common structure. That structure is helpful to both the writer—who wants to know what to cover—and the reader—who knows what to expect. We cover that structure in three basic parts: the front end, the body of the report, and the back end. The front end of a report covers all material up to the actual body of the report (e.g., the cover page, table of contents, and executive summary). Usually developed at the end of the actual writing of the report, the elements of the front end are, nevertheless, extremely important to the report's success. The body of the report covers the actual discussion of the project itself. It includes an introduction, major sections and subsections of the report's content, the report's conclusions and recommendations, and the reference section. The back end of the report includes all the support material for the report in appropriate appendices.

It is important to remember that project reports are technical documents. There is little glamour and creativity to them. Clear and concise writing is the goal. Almost never are they narratives. They do not tell stories; they simply report findings of the project.[5] The reader does not need to know, for example, all the possible actions the project team could have taken along the way. The reader simply needs to know the important ones actually taken and relevant results. Project reports are not marketing documents, either. Even project proposals should reject marketing ploys and gimmicks. Project teams should let the quality of the project report speak for itself. If the proposal or report addresses the needs of the stakeholder in a clear, appropriate, and competent way, the project will sell itself.

All this is not to say that authors should ignore the packaging and presentation of the report. In addition to the technical requirements of report writing (clear concise statements, appropriate use of headings and bullets, appropriate macrostructure of content, and the like), the look of a report also matters. Graphics and illustrations should be pleasing to the eye. Support appendices are often bound separately from the front end and body of the report. This allows the report itself to be read and transported more easily and makes the smaller main report itself look more accessible to a reader than a 6- or 8-inch-thick report that includes appendices. Such elements do count for making the report more readable, but in the end, a project report is meant simply to present and explain facts and outcomes of the project.

THE FRONT END

The **front end of a report** includes its cover page, possibly a letter of transmittal, a table of contents, lists of tables and illustrations, and the executive summary. Each of these begins on a new page.

The Cover Page

The **cover page** of a project report is straightforward. It begins with the title of the report, gives the authors' names and titles (sometimes this is an organization rather than a person or team), provides the date of transmittal, and includes the names of the people or organization receiving the report.[6]

The title of the project is often the title of the report. Tim and Jennifer's report, for example, might be titled "Final Report on the Feasibility of Establishing Manufacturing and Marketing Operations in China." At least two common mistakes occur in providing titles. First, some writers want to capture all the elements of a project in its title, which results in a title several lines long (e.g., "Final Report on the Feasibility of Developing Manufacturing Operations in China Inclusive of Supply Chain Considerations, Cost Parameters, and Cultural Aspects as Well as Marketing...." Well, you get the idea.). Although accuracy is achieved, the reader knows from the very start that reading the report will be a difficult task. Other writers will often give a report a catchy title in hopes of grabbing the attention of the reader or simply expressing their own creativity. "On Gaining a Foothold in the Mysterious Orient" or a similar title may or may not pique the interest of some readers, but it tells very little about what is inside the report.

The Letter of Transmittal

The **letter of transmittal** is used to convey the project report to a specific reader, group, or audience. It usually follows the normal layout and conventions of a business letter or memo. Opening remarks usually identify the project to the reader. Letters for final reports usually state that the terms of the contract have been met and present one or two key findings or outcomes that are of key interest to the recipient of the letter. It is a good idea to formally acknowledge the help of key stakeholders of the project—particularly those who funded it. Offers of future help might be included (to encourage future business) and contact information provided in case the reader has questions or would like your team to work with him or her in the future. The letter of transmittal may or may not be bound with the report itself, and it is important to note that one report may warrant multiple letters of transmittal. Different recipients may require slightly different versions, each focusing on their particular interests in the report or project.

The Table of Contents

The **table of contents** lists the major sections and subsections of the report along with the page numbers where they can be found.[7] The table of contents begins on a separate page with the title of the report at the top followed by the title "Table of Contents."

Beyond the technical requirements of the table of contents (e.g., getting the headings and page numbers right), a table of contents plays a very important role in any project report. Consider for a moment where you first look to see what is inside a book or larger report. It is almost always the table of contents. Because the table of contents is where the reader will look first, it provides the writer with an opportunity let the reader know what is in the report that will be of interest to him or her. It also provides the reader with a quick overview of the report and a map to its contents. With these ideas in mind, the headings used in the report and given in the table of contents should be clear, concise, and descriptive of the content covered underneath the heading. As with the title of the report itself, overly long technical headings and vague catchy ones are to be avoided.

Lists of Tables and Illustrations

Project reports also contain **lists of tables and illustrations** that appear in the report. These are listed separately from one another, have their own titles (e.g., "List of Tables"), and provide the page numbers where the tables and illustrations can be found.[8]

The Executive Summary

The **executive summary** is one of the most important components of any project report. A great deal of attention should be given to it. The label "executive summary" conveys the essence of what is being written and for whom. The summary is designed principally for decision makers. Generally, these include those who have funded the project and those who will decide what, if any, actions are to be taken based on it. Writers should keep their needs in mind when producing the executive summary (see "What Decision Makers Want," covered previously). Quite often, decision makers read little else besides the executive summary and the report's conclusions and recommendations.

The term *summary* in an executive summary refers to a summary of the project's outcomes or findings. Rarely does this include how the project was done unless the conduct of the project was an integral part of the project itself (e.g., using a particular required approach to a study). Even in these cases, the conduct of the project would be summarized only briefly (e.g., "Using prescribed methods....").

Recall what decision makers generally want to read. The executive summary begins with a very brief introduction of background information: the purpose and objectives of the project along with other information required to help focus the decision maker on what the project was all about. This should take about a short paragraph. The remainder of the executive summary should summarize the important findings and outcomes of the project.

It should conclude with a few of the project's key conclusions and recommendations, if any. In general, the executive summary is best kept to a single page, although an executive summary of less than a page that adequately addresses the project is even better. More involved projects may require more than a page.

Because executive summaries are summaries of outcomes for decision makers, they generally do not cover descriptions of the process to develop the outcome or relate stories of who did what. Being necessarily brief, summaries do not say explicitly that any of their content is important—it is assumed to be important because it is in the summary. Finally, executive summaries are not venues for advertising how well the project was done or how important its outcomes are to the reader. Given the proper presentation of the facts and outcomes, the reader will see that the project not only was done well but achieved its aims without any sales pitch.

THE BODY

The **body of the report** begins on a new page with the title of the report at the top. It begins with the report's introduction, moves through the major sections and subsections of the report, wraps up with the report's conclusions and recommendations, and ends with the reference section.

The Introduction

The introduction of the report provides at least two key background elements of the project. The first is the purpose and objectives of the project and any key information related to them (e.g., for whom the project was done, key constraints). The introductory statement given in the executive summary can be duplicated and elaborated a little more here. A good, serviceable start for an introduction is a **purpose statement** that mirrors the project's mission statement: "The purpose of this project was to . . ."

The second element of an introduction is the project's **scope statement**. This would include the project's main objectives and its specific deliverables. A general overview of the project scope is enough for the body of the report with any more required detail given in a supporting appendix. Although most readers generally skim or skip this material, it is a formal statement of what was required and delivered for the project. As we will see in a little more detail below, the scope statement for Tim and Jennifer's China Report would include project objectives related to the investigation and assessments of operations related to manufacturing and marketing of Tech Machine products—deliverables the project was supposed to produce.

Major Sections and Subsections of the Report

The major sections and subsections of the report follow and, together, form the "macrostructure" of the report. The **macrostructure** is the overall organizational structure of the report's body, which allows it to flow logically from one topic to the next. A well-planned macrostructure allows the reader to easily navigate and understand the main objectives and topics of the report and, therefore, the project itself. Quite often, the project's main objectives and deliverables can help the writer develop the report's macrostructure. The major objectives of the project might be used to structure the **major sections** of the report, and **subsections** might deal with second-level objectives or deliverables. In this case, the scope statement given in the introduction can serve as an overview of the report's content. The key here is to "chunk" information in ways that make sense. The structure of the project itself can help writers do just that.

In Tim and Jennifer's report, for example, the body of the report might be broken down into two major sections: "Developing Manufacturing Operations" and "Developing Marketing Operations." Looking into the feasibility of these two ventures were the basic objectives of their project. Subobjectives and deliverables in each of those areas, then, would likely form subsections of the report. For example, when looking into manufacturing operations, Tim and Jennifer may have been charged to consider (a) possible locations, (b) the skilled and unskilled labor market, (c) issues related to the acquisition of plant and materials, and (d) the costs of such an endeavor. Subsections devoted to each of these, then, would be appropriate. A similar structure would be appropriate for the marketing objectives and requirements of the project.

The structure and layout of each section and subsection should promote skimming. Descriptive headings in bold font help the reader quickly identify the location and contents of the sections and subsections of interest to him or her. In each section, information is best chunked into coherent units of related information. For example, each subsection should deal only with related issues, each paragraph with one basic idea. Bullets with descriptive labels (also in bold font) can help the reader identify content of interest quickly.

The body of the report should go into enough detail to cover the issues adequately but leave extensive details and large listings of data to supportive appendices. Admittedly, this can be a tricky call, and knowing what the most important readers want will help the writer. In general, though, the body of the report seeks to explain project outcomes—not review lots of data and detail. Concise summaries of information and data in tables and graphs are handy ways of presenting supporting facts and figures. Supportive appendices with more detailed data are identified in the body of the report when the issues are covered. References to appendices should use the name of the appendix and give the page number where the appendix can be found.[9]

Conclusions and Recommendations

Conclusions and recommendations wrap up the report and are one of its most important sections. After reading the executive summary and, perhaps, giving the body of the report a quick scan, many decision makers turn to this section for extended reading and consideration.

Although the conclusions and recommendations of a project are reserved for a relatively small section of the report, they represent some of the most important products the team can provide. The project team has been deeply involved in all aspects of a project of great interest to the client. Only the project team has had full access to all the issues, information, problems, and solutions in the project. The project team, then, is in the best position to analyze the project's results, come to conclusions about them, and make recommendations to further the client's aims. This section, then, represents one of the most important value-added components of a project, and it requires careful and extended thought.

Conclusions summarize the findings and outcomes of the project, not the content of the report itself—a common mistake. Now that the project is done, what did you find out or discover? What can you conclude about the project's objectives? This section calls on the project leader and team to analyze the project and its objectives and outcomes. Now that they have the experience of the project behind them, what can the project team conclude that is of value to the client, decision maker, or other reader? Tim and Jennifer, for example, might offer conclusions about the initial problems the company might face in setting up manufacturing operations. Conclusions about initial costs, revenue projections, payback period, and critical issues that need to be addressed if the venture is to be successful might also be covered.

Recommendations are courses of action that the project team suggests decision makers should take. Recall that decision makers are paid to make things happen. Your recommendations, then, should be clear, concrete, and action-oriented. Tim and Jennifer, for example, might recommend a specific location to set up manufacturing operations and specific vendors to fill the company's needs for equipment and material. They might go on to recommend a number of businesses to approach first as potential buyers of Tech Machine products and recommend different distribution channels.

These kinds of recommendations are both concrete and action-oriented. Like project objectives, when recommendations are specific, concrete, and actionable, they become useful to decision makers.

References

Most projects most often use some sources of support for their work. Books, journals, articles, and government documents are a few examples. People contacted and websites are others. The **reference section** is where these materials are listed. The reference section is usually one of the last sections developed for a project report. By that time, the sources and citations used in a project are often long-gone and forgotten. It is important, therefore, to keep a running list of support material as the project moves forward in one centralized location. Whether or not you are required to stick close to some citation format (e.g., MLA or APA), it is important to list sources in a standardized way so that they can be located (author, title, publication date, etc.).

Most decision makers are not too concerned with the reference section. Expert advisors, on the other hand, may well review this section very carefully. They want to make sure you have considered and used all the required, important, and up-to-date studies and sources in the project's area of work. The credibility of the project team and its work can be influenced by the extent to which experts favorably review its sources. Those who will use or implement some or all of the report's recommendations can find the reference section useful as well for their follow-up work. Keeping these readers in mind, writers also may include sources they have come across—but did not incorporate into the report itself—because implementers might find them useful (e.g., how-to manuals, instruments, government documents, and important contacts). Writers can help users as well by providing short annotations of their sources: one- to three-sentence descriptions relevant to user interests. These small efforts can provide real value-added at little to no cost to the project team.

THE BACK END: SUPPORTING APPENDICES

The **back end of a report** contains all the support material of a project report in appropriate appendices. Those **appendices** contain detailed information for the final report. They include as well material that might have been mandated by the project but is inappropriate or too detailed for inclusion into the body of the report. The project may have been required, for example, to conduct certain studies. The details of those studies might well be included as appendices so expert advisors can review their quality. Often, projects require the development of material in anticipation of follow-up work (e.g., work procedures or technical manuals). That material is part of the product of the project, and its delivery is often included in the appendices of a report. Finally, the project team may come across useful material as a by-product of its project work (e.g., checklists, questionnaires, operating procedures, schematics, or instruction manuals). These would provide value added to the project's results and would also be included in the report's appendices.

Table 9.1 includes a list of questions project report writers might find useful. It can serve as a check-off list for some of the major components of more formal project reports. Although not exhaustive of all considerations, it can serve as an initial point of departure.

Table 9.1   Project Report Check-Off List

There are any number of reports that need to be written for a project. Final reports, progress reports, and proposals are just a few, but it is important to keep in mind that many aspects of these reports overlap. Listed here are a few key questions project leaders might ask themselves as they move through the process of writing a more formal, end-of-project report. The questions are meant to encourage project leaders to think through the issues involved and to be used as a point of departure rather than as a comprehensive listing.

- Is the title of the report descriptive of its contents?
- Does the table of contents give a good overview of the report? Are the section headings descriptive of their contents? Does the table help the reader to skim the section headings? Can the reader quickly find material that is of interest to him or her?
- Does the executive summary open with a one- or two-sentence description of the project? Does the rest of the summary provide a quick overview of the project's major findings, conclusions, and recommendations? Give serious consideration to excluding all other material from the executive summary.
- Does the introduction of the report provide a quick description of the project? Is a scope statement included listing the major deliverables of the project?
- Is the body of the report arranged in a logical order? Are the section headings descriptive of their contents? Is the report written to facilitate skimming, so the reader can quickly understand the main issues and focus on those of interest to him or her? Consider the use of bulleted lists where helpful. Consider the use of graphs to display data. Does the report use jargon that intended readers will not understand? Is there too much detail given anywhere.

(Continued)

Table 9.1 (Continued)

in the body? If so, consider moving it to a supporting appendix and providing an overview summary in the body of the report.

- Do the conclusions focus on what has been learned from the project—what can be concluded from it? Are the conclusions clear and logical? Do the conclusions address all issues the client wanted? Resist using the conclusion section to summarize the report itself. If you want a report summary, consider using a separate section for it (e.g., "Report Summary").
- Do the recommendations address all issues the client wanted? Are they action-oriented—do they help decision makers make action decisions?
- Does the reference section contain references to key material required for the project? Would an expert advisor see those sources needed for the project listed? If the report is to be used as an aid in implementation activities, are sources useful for implementation included?
- Do the technical appendices include everything that was contracted as a deliverable? Are supportive data and information included? Consider including low-cost information that would be helpful to your client.

SUMMARY

Project reports come in all shapes and sizes. Our focus has been on the larger formal report that is given to a client at the project's end. Many of the elements found in those reports are also found in others.

The most important thing authors need to remember about writing project reports is to keep the needs of their readers in mind. The average reader wants the report to state things simply and clearly and to have ready and quick access to information he or she sees as important. Project leaders want readers to have confidence in their abilities as well. How the project is presented in its final report can go a long way toward that end. Decision makers want project reports to help them make decisions about the action objectives that are facing them. They want a quick review of the project's background and information that speaks to the strategic issues facing them. It is best to layer project information so decision makers can access more and more detail as they desire. It is best to avoid technical jargon when writing for decision makers and make sure to write to their level of expertise. Decision makers often look to expert advisors to assess the quality of the project's information. Advisors will want to know that the project team has covered the important sources for the project and will want access to detailed information about it. That level of detail is usually provided in the project report's appendices. Projects are also read by those who are charged with implementing their recommendations. Project leaders should consider such implementers as project stakeholders and produce material useful for them and their activities. Often, this material is placed in the report's appendices as well. To the extent a project is to serve as a first step among many, implementers become a more important stakeholder, and the project needs to include their needs in initial project planning and cost calculations.

Formal project reports have a similar structure: a front end, a main body, and a back end. The front end consists of the cover page, the letter of transmittal, the table of contents, lists of tables and illustrations, and the executive summary. The cover page includes the title, the name of who is submitting it, and the submission date. The title should be brief but simple and descriptive of the report's content. The letter of transmittal formally transmits the report to the client and is written much like a business letter or memo. The table of contents is more than a mere listing of section headings. It is the place readers turn to first when looking over a report to assess its content quickly. Writers should make sure that the section headings used in the body of the report and listed in the table of contents are simple and descriptive of the issues covered. Lists of tables and illustrations indicate where in the report those tables and illustrations are located. The executive summary is one of the most important components of a final report. It summarizes the most important outcomes of the project, and decision makers often depend on it alone for most of their information.

The body of the report includes the introduction, the main sections and subsections of the report, its conclusions and recommendations, and the reference section. The introduction should open with the purpose of the project and a statement of its scope: its principal objectives and deliverables. The main sections of the report will often parallel the major and minor objectives of the project itself, reporting findings and outcomes relevant to them. It is important to chunk information in each section so that subsections address connected issues. The general purpose of the main body of a report is not to present the project's detail but to review its findings and explain them to the reader. Although facts and figures are given in the main body, detailed information is best left to supporting appendices. Conclusions and recommendations form a small part of the report but present some of its most important information—what the project team concludes about the project and its objectives given their deep involvement with them and their recommendations about what should be done next. Conclusions are conclusions about project outcomes—not summaries of the report itself. Recommendations should be specific, concrete, and action-oriented.

Although decision makers often do not pay attention to the reference section, expert advisors and implementers do. Advisors want to see if the project team has covered and used the material they should have. Implementers would like sources cited that will help them implement the report's recommendations.

The back end of a project report contains all of its supportive appendices. These include specific products mandated as project deliverables, details of project activities that may need to be reviewed for quality assurance, and any material that the project team may have come across in the course of its work that might be useful for the client. Often, the appendices are bound separately from the main report itself. Some specific appendices may even be bound separately themselves to help readers use them (e.g., manuals produced for later use by implementers).

REVIEW QUESTIONS

1. Different readers want different things from a project report.

   a. What does any reader want?

   b. Compare and contrast what decision makers and expert advisors want in a project report.

   c. What do users or those who will implement a report want to see in it?

2. Discuss the importance of the executive summary and what it should and should not contain.

3. Other than indicating where content is located, what function does the table of contents play for the reader?

   a. What considerations should be given to the section titles contained in a table of contents?

4. What are some of the considerations in developing the major sections of the project report's body?

5. What issues are covered in the project report's conclusions and recommendations?

6. What material is typically contained in a project report's supporting appendices?

EXERCISES

1. Locate a recent student paper you or some friend has written or a paper produced by one of your professors.

a. Write an executive summary of the paper.

b. Produce a table of contents for the paper following the guidelines in this chapter. You may have to develop titles for the various sections of the paper. Does the table of contents reveal the substantive content of the paper?

2. Identify any project in which you played a role. This can be a project done for a class or work assignment, a project for a school organization, or one that you developed on your own.

a. Write an executive summary of the project. Review the summary to see if it reveals what a decision maker would want to know.

b. If you were to write a report of the project, what sections would be in the body of the report? Label those sections so that they would reveal what the project was about when placed in a table of contents.

c. Consider what you can conclude from your project and write up a small conclusions section.

d. If someone else were to repeat your project, what would be your recommendations? Write them up in a small section.

ENDNOTES

1. Although roles such as these are common ones, William Pfeiffer does a good job of reviewing them. His detailed handling of all kinds of reports makes his work an excellent reference as well. See Pfeiffer, W. (2003). *Technical writing: A practical approach* (5th ed.). Upper Saddle River, NJ: Prentice Hall. Another excellent book, by William Zinsser, shows quite clearly that even technical reports can be written in an engaging way. See Zinsser, W. (1998). *On writing well: The classic guide to writing nonfiction*. New York, NY: HarperCollins.

2. I recall one presentation put together by some exceptionally talented technical experts in the field of project risk analysis. The presentation was delivered to some key NATO decision makers about a particular technique for assessing project risk. The presentation had some 47 PowerPoint© slides, beginning with some basic concepts developed by ancient Greeks! Death by PowerPoint© is often matched in a parallel fashion in written reports. Decision makers want you to get to the point quickly with information they see as important.

3. Most word processing programs allow for the insertion of appendix titles and page numbers in the body of a report that will automatically update as they change.

4. Sometimes such follow-on work is a major part and cost item of a project. In the design and production of weapon systems for the military, for example, specification for equipment maintenance is a very large component.

5. There are exceptions, of course. The 9/11 Commission Report, for example, incorporates narratives because its intended readership includes the American people, who would find them engaging as well as informative: National Commission on

Terrorist Attacks. (2004). *9/11 commission report: Final report of the National Commission on Terrorist Attacks Upon the United States.* New York, NY: Norton.

6. It is often the case that a report will go through a number of drafts and be shared with a number of people to get their feedback. In such cases, it is a good idea to include the report's file name and date of last revision or printing in the footer of the cover page. This information will be updated automatically as the report goes through its revisions, and it can be removed with the report's final printing. This is a practice that writers will grow to love.

7. All modern word processors have the capability of scanning for section headings in the report if the headings are properly identified. In Microsoft Word©, for example, first- and lower-order headings can be specified as styles, with each heading given its own label. The same can be done with titles of illustrations, tables or figures, and the like. The key benefit of this is that the word processing program can automatically generate the table of contents inclusive of all headings and their current page locations. Moreover, when changes are made, the program can automatically update the changes into the table of contents. Being able to specify and work with these kinds of headings is an ability well worth developing for any writer.

8. As with the headings of sections in the table of contents, the titles used for tables and illustrations in the report can have a style associated with them so that they will automatically be presented in their respective lists with appropriate page numbers.

9. Again, most word processing programs allow for this kind of page linking as with headings in the table of contents.

KEY TERMS

Appendices: detailed support material at the end of a project report. This includes information required by the project that was too detailed to include in the body of the report as well as other value-added information that the project team encountered or produced during project work.

Back End of a Report: contains all the support material of a project report in appropriate appendices.

Background Information: a brief explanation of the problem that the project addresses as well as the basic objectives of the project. Background information should be included in the executive summary as well as in the introduction to the project report.

Body of a Report: the main text of a project report, which includes an introduction, the major sections and subsections of the report, and the conclusions and recommendations, followed by the reference section.

Conclusions: discusses the findings and outcomes of the project. The conclusions section establishes what the project team concluded by way of the project—what was found out or discovered.

Decision Makers: those who have the authority to allocate resources to a project and to follow up on any recommendations the report makes. They tend to be very busy and usually focus their attention on the executive summary as well as the conclusions and recommendations sections of a project report.

Executive Summary: a brief summary of the project report, written with decision makers' needs in mind. This includes a brief reminder of the project's purpose and objectives followed by the project's key findings, conclusions, and recommendations.

Expert Advisors: readers who are often relied upon by decision makers to confirm the quality of a project report's content, they expect thorough explanations and detailed data to support the report's conclusions. This extra detail often can appear in appendices.

Front End of a Report: the first part of the project report, which includes the cover page, the letter of transmittal, the table of contents, lists of tables and illustrations, and the executive summary.

Implementers: readers who will use the report to carry out some or all of the recommendations made in the report or implement other decisions based on the report.

Letter of Transmittal: conveys the report to a specific reader, group, or audience. It may or may not be bound with the report itself, and one report may warrant multiple letters of transmittal for different recipients.

Lists of Tables and Illustrations: list the tables and illustrations that appear in the report and the page numbers where they can be found.

Macrostructure: the overall organizational structure of the report's body, which allows it to flow logically from one topic to the next. It determines the major sections and subsections of the report and is often based on the main objectives and deliverables of the project.

Major Sections: first-level, main sections of the body of the project report. These sections are often structured around the project's main objectives.

Purpose Statement: a clear statement of the project's main purpose. As background information, it is often the lead component of the introduction of a project report.

Recommendations: courses of action that the project team suggests to decision makers based upon the report's conclusions. Recommendations should be clear, concrete, and action-oriented.

Reference Section: a list of the external sources used for the project report, such as books, journals, articles, government documents, websites, and people contacted.

Scope Statement: a formal statement of what was expected and delivered by the project. It includes the project's main objectives and its specific deliverables.

Subsections: second-level sections of the body of the project report commonly structured around specific deliverables or stages of the project within each major section or objective.

Table of Contents: lists all sections and subsections of the report along with their page numbers. Not only does it allow the reader to quickly navigate the report, but it also provides a quick overview of the report's content.

Appendix A

Calculating the Critical Path Using the Critical Path Method

As the name suggests, the Critical Path Method was designed to help determine the critical path in a network diagram. In addition, it points out the slack in all the tasks that are not on the critical path. The critical path and task slack are determined with a forward and backward pass through the network. For example, Figure A.1 presents Dr. Howard's study given in Chapter 4. Each node in the network is represented by a box. The box contains the task number, name, and time estimate in the upper half. In the lower half of each node are spaces for the earliest and latest start dates for the task and its earliest and latest finish dates.

In Figure A.1, we see the results of a forward pass through the project network. The earliest start date for the first task (3.1 [Assemble Test]) is 0—the start of the project. Because it will take 3 days to complete, its earliest finish date is 3—3 days into the project. All succeeding tasks build on this and other task time requirements. For example, the earliest start date for 3.3 [Experiment 2: Stage 1] is Day 3 following the earliest finish date of the task on which it depends. Task 3.3 will take 4 days to complete, so its earliest finish date is 7 days into the project.

Whenever two or more task streams come together, as they do when connecting with 3.8 [Analyze Data], the *latest* "early finish" date of all preceding tasks is chosen for the earliest start date for the succeeding task. It does not matter, for example, that the Stage 2s for Experiments 1 and 3 finish 8 and 6 days into the project. Analyzing Data still cannot begin until Stage 2 of Experiment 2 ends on Day 9—the latest "early finish" date of the three tasks.

This procedure continues until the last task of the project. In Figure A.1, that task is 3.9 [Write Report]. The earliest it can begin is on Day 13 of the project. It will take 10 days to complete, finishing the project 23 days after it was begun.

The backward pass of the critical path method nails down the critical path and calculates the slack of all noncritical tasks. The backward pass begins with the last day of the last task of the project. Figure A.2 is the same as Figure A.1 except the earliest start and finish dates have been removed for purposes of presentation. The latest finish date for the project's last task is set to its earliest finish date. Now, going backward, task times are subtracted from the project's timeline. The latest start date for 3.9 [Writing Report], for example, must be Day 13 if the project is to be completed by the 23rd day.

When two or more tasks branch out from a task, the latest start date of the task before the branch is given as the latest finish dates to each of them. The second stages of all three experiments, for example, have until Day 9 to finish and still allow Task 3.8 [Analyze Data] to begin on time for project completion. This same procedure is followed until the backward pass is complete, ending with the project's first task.

Figure A.3 displays all the information developed on both the forward and backward passes through the project network and indicates the critical path with thick-lined arrows. Note that the earliest and latest start and finish dates on the critical path are the same. All of them must start and finish on time or the whole project timeline gets moved. Tasks off the critical path show the slack or float for each task. For example, Task 3.4 [Experiment 3: Stage 1], can start on the 6th day of the project and still finish in time so Stage 2 will not push back the data analysis in Task 3.8.

The critical path method provides a straightforward, commonsense procedure for critical path calculations. The forward pass calculates when the earliest project tasks can begin and end; the backward pass calculates the latest times. When those are the same for any task, it lies on the critical path. When those are different, the task lies off the critical path and provides slack for the project. As projects grow in size and complexity, project management software greatly facilitates these calculations.

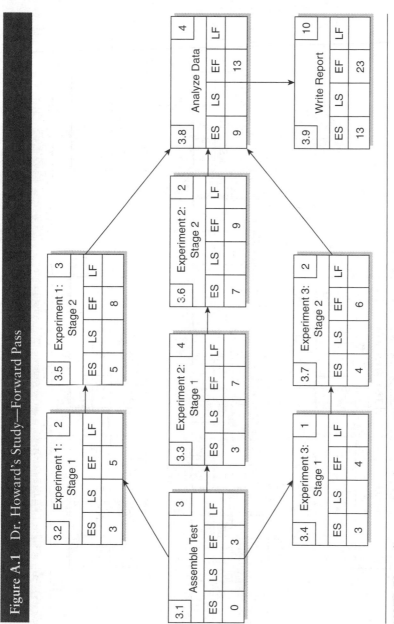

Figure A.1   Dr. Howard's Study—Forward Pass

NOTE: ES = earliest start; LS = latest start; EF = earliest finish; LF = latest finish.

Figure A.2   Dr. Howard's Study—Backward Pass

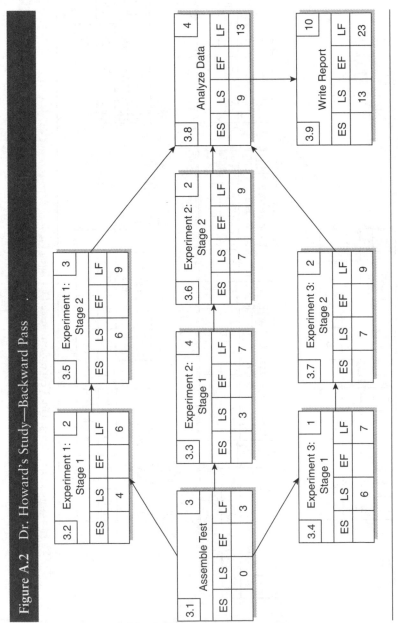

NOTE: ES = earliest start; LS = latest start; EF = earliest finish; LF = latest finish.

Figure A.3 Dr. Howard's Study Showing All Start and Finish Dates and the Critical Path

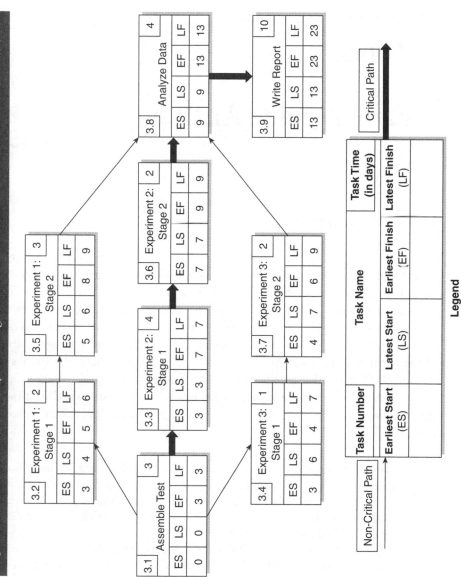

Appendix B

Earned Value Analysis

INTRODUCTION

Earned value analysis is an accounting tool used to help assess the extent to which a project is on schedule and on budget—it marries the time and costs of a project. The components of earned value analysis include planned value, earned value, and actual costs. Planned value and earned value use planned costs to measure the project's progress—the extent to which the project is on schedule or not. They do so by calculating the differences between the money that was planned to be spent (planned value) versus the planned money actually spent (earned value). Actual costs versus planned costs are used to assess whether the project is on budget. This is discussed in more detail below, starting with the components of planned value, earned value, and actual costs.

- **Planned value:** This refers to the budgeted costs of work *scheduled* for a project. Recall that in project planning, the costs of all project tasks are estimated and budgeted. Each task has a planned value, then, and the sum total of all those tasks is the "planned value" of the project as a whole—the dollar total of all budgeted project tasks.

  At any one point in the life of a project, a certain number of tasks are scheduled to be completed. The planned value of the project to that point is the total dollar value of budgeted tasks that were supposed to be done. The planned value of a project as it proceeds through its life cycle establishes the "baseline" for the project—what *should* have been spent at any particular time in the project. It serves as the key reference point for project calculations.

- **Earned value:** This refers to the *budgeted* cost of work actually performed on a project (*not* the actual costs—an important distinction). At any point between a project's start and its end, a certain number of tasks will have been completed. The sum total of budgeted costs for those completed tasks is that part of the project's "planned value" the project has actually "earned"—its "earned value." If the total budgeted costs of work completed—or earned—is *more* than what was planned for by that time, it means that the project is ahead of schedule. (Because more tasks have actually been completed than planned, the budgeted costs "earned" will be more than what was planned for at that point in the project.) If the budgeted costs of tasks actually completed—or earned—are *less* than planned for by that time, it means that the project is behind schedule (the tasks done to date have "earned" less than planned).
- **Actual cost:** This is the total of all actual costs of work performed in a project by a certain date. If actual costs are more than planned, the project is over budget; if less, then the project is under budget.

EARNED VALUE CALCULATIONS

Earned value calculations use planned value, earned value, and actual cost to help monitor the progress and costs of a project. Earned value versus planned value is a measure of whether the project is ahead, behind, or on schedule (also known as "schedule variance"). Actual project costs versus earned value (i.e., the *budgeted* costs of work performed) is a measure of whether a project is over, under, or on budget (also known as "cost variance").[1]

Table B.1 shows various earned value calculations for a project that we will use in our discussion. At first, the table can be a little overwhelming. As we go through it, though, the "facts and figures" begin to fall into place.

For the moment, refer to the upper part of B.1. What we see is a Gantt chart of a project with five tasks (1.0 through 5.0) scheduled to be completed in 11 weeks. On the right side, we see Gantt chart bars showing the schedule for those five tasks. The heavy line at the end of Week 8 indicates that we are just ending the 8th week of the project. In between the tasks and the bar chart, we see the budgeted costs for each of the five tasks. For purposes of this example, those costs are distributed equally across the weeks each task is planned to take before completion. The weekly costs for each task are shown in their respective Gantt chart bars.

Just below the Gantt chart bars, we see two cost calculations. In the first row are the "Budgeted costs of work scheduled for each week" for all 11 weeks. In the second row, those same costs are added up as the project is scheduled to move forward. Those cumulative costs represent the *planned value* of the project as it moves through time. Those planned costs serve as

Table B.1 Planned Value, Earned Value, and Actual Costs

Gantt Chart Showing 5 Tasks and their Weekly Costs: Project is at end of Eighth Week		Week											
Task	Budgeted Costs per Task	1	2	3	4	5	6	7	8	9	10	11
1.0	$4,000	$1,000	$1,000	$1,000	$1,000							
2.0	$2,500			$500	$500	$500	$500	$500				
3.0	$9,000				$1,500	$1,500	$1,500	$1,500	$1,500	$1,500		
4.0	$5,000						$1,000	$1,000	$1,000	$1,000	$1,000	
5.0	$1,500									$500	$500	$500
Budgeted costs of work scheduled for each week		$1,000	$1,000	$1,500	$3,000	$2,000	$3,000	$3,000	$2,500	$3,000	$1,500	$500
Planned Value: Cumulative of budgeted costs of work scheduled—a project's baseline		$1,000	$2,000	$3,500	$6,500	$8,500	$11,500	$14,500	$17,000	$20,000	$21,500	$22,000

(Continued)

Table B.1 (Continued—Weeks 1 to 8 only)

			Number of Weeks into the Project					
	1	2	3	4	5	6	7	8
Schedule Scenarios: Earned Value vs. Planned Value (also see Figure B.1)								
Planned Value: Cumulative budgeted costs of work scheduled	$1,000	$2,000	$3,500	$6,500	$8,500	$11,500	$14,500	$17,000
Earned Value: Ahead of schedule	$1,000	$3,000	$5,500	$9,000	$11,500	$16,000	$19,500	$21,000
Schedule variance is positive*	$0	$1,000	$2,000	$2,500	$3,000	$4,500	$5,000	$4,000
Earned Value: Behind schedule	$1,000	$1,500	$2,500	$5,000	$6,200	$8,500	$11,000	$13,000
Schedule variance is negative	$0	($500)	($1,000)	($1,500)	($2,300)	($3,000)	($3,500)	($4,000)
Cost Scenarios: Earned Value vs. Actual Costs								
Earned Value: Ahead of Schedule (also see Figure B.2)	$1,000	$3,000	$5,500	$9,000	$11,500	$16,000	$19,500	$21,000
Actual costs are more than planned.	$1,000	$4,000	$6,500	$10,500	$14,000	$19,500	$24,000	$26,500
Cost Variance is negative**	$0	($1,000)	($1,000)	($1,500)	($2,500)	($3,500)	($4,500)	($5,500)
Actual costs are less than planned.	$1,000	$2,500	$4,500	$7,500	$10,000	$14,000	$16,500	$18,000
Cost variance is positive	$0	$500	$1,000	$1,500	$1,500	$2,000	$3,000	$3,000
Earned Value: Behind Schedule (also see Figure B.3)	$1,000	$1,500	$2,500	$5,000	$6,200	$8,500	$11,000	$13,000
Actual costs are more than planned.	$1,000	$1,700	$2,900	$6,000	$6,900	$9,700	$12,500	15,300
Cost variance is negative	$0	($200)	($400)	($1,000)	($700)	($1,200)	($1,500)	($2,300)
Actual costs are less than planned.	$1,000	$1,300	$2,100	$4,200	$5,200	$7,200	$9,500	$11,800
Cost variance is positive	$0	$200	$400	$800	$1,000	$1,300	$1,500	$1,200

NOTES: *Schedule variance = Earned value − Planned value

**Cost variance = Earned value − Actual costs

a nice point of reference for the project and is referred to as the *project's cost baseline* or, more simply, the *project's baseline*.

Schedule Variance

Schedule variance is the difference between the earned value (EV) of work *actually* performed and the planned value (PV) of work *scheduled* to be performed or (SV = EV – PV). A positive variance is usually thought of as good; it means that the work actually performed is ahead of the work scheduled to be performed. A negative variance is usually not so good, the work actually performed is behind the work scheduled to be performed.

Just below the Gantt chart in Table B.1 we see different "Schedule Scenarios: Earned Value vs. Planned Value." The first row shows "Planned Value: Cumulative budgeted costs of work scheduled" for the first 8 weeks. These are the total costs that *should* have been spent each of the first 8 weeks according to plan. The next two rows show the first scenario—what happens when tasks are done sooner than expected. "Earned Value: Ahead of schedule" shows that the budgeted costs of project tasks have been "earned" more quickly than planned. This results in a positive variance for the schedule (i.e., "Schedule variance is positive"), showing that the project is ahead of schedule.

The second scenario shows what happens when tasks are completed later than expected. "Earned Value: Behind schedule" shows that the budgeted costs of project tasks actually completed have been "earned" more slowly than scheduled in the plan. This results in a "Schedule variance [that] is negative," indicating that the project is behind schedule.

Both these scenarios are shown in Figure B.1: "Earned Value Versus Planned Value (Baseline)." The graph shows how these positive and negative values for earned value compare to the project's baseline of planned value.

Cost Variance

Cost variance—the extent to which the project is over or under budget—compares actual costs to *earned* value—*not* planned value. That is because if the project were ahead of schedule, we would expect the actual costs to be more than what was planned by that date because the work actually performed (and earned) is ahead of what was planned. If the project were behind schedule, on the other hand, we would expect actual costs earned to be less than what were planned.

Below the "Schedule Scenarios" are the "Cost Scenarios: Earned Value Versus Actual Costs." The first set of cost scenarios focus on actual costs

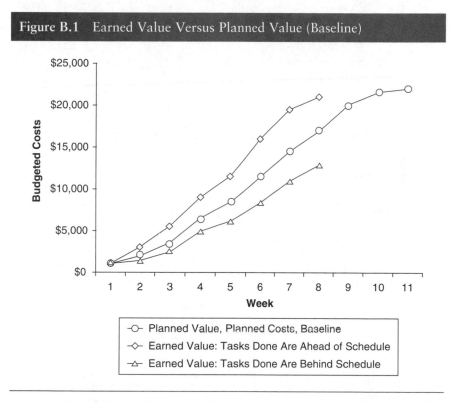

Figure B.1   Earned Value Versus Planned Value (Baseline)

when "Earned Value [is] Ahead of Schedule"—budgeted costs are being "earned" faster than scheduled.

The first cost scenario in the next two rows show what happens when "Actual costs are more than planned" for the work completed and the "Cost variance is negative." Here the project is ahead of schedule but over budget. Nice on the one hand, not so good on the other.

The second cost scenario in the next two rows show what happens when "Actual costs are less than planned" for completed work and "Cost variance is positive." Here the project is ahead of schedule and under budget—a nice position to be in! Figure B.2: "Actual Costs While Ahead of Schedule" shows those scenarios graphically. Figure B.2 has the same planned value baseline as Figure B.1 and the same earned value line that shows the project ahead of schedule. We have added to it actual costs illustrating a project over and under budget.

The second set of cost scenarios show actual costs when the work done is behind schedule. The first row, "Earned Value: Behind schedule," shows the earned value figures to be *less* than the planned value figures under the Gantt chart.

Figure B.2   Actual Costs While Ahead of Schedule

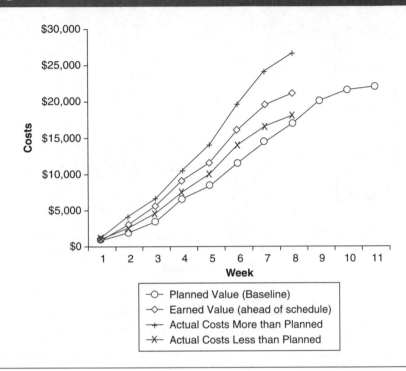

The third cost scenario in the next two rows again shows what happens when "Actual costs are more than planned" for the work completed and "Cost variance is negative." Here the project is both behind schedule *and* over budget—not a great position!

The final cost scenario in the following two rows show that "Actual costs are less than planned," with the result that "Cost variance is positive." The project is still behind schedule, but at least actual costs are less than budgeted—again, a mixture of good and bad news. Figure B.3: "Actual Costs While Behind Schedule" shows those scenarios graphically with the same baseline and "behind schedule" earned value as in Figure B.1. We have added actual costs that represent a project over and under budget to it.

USES OF EARNED VALUE ANALYSIS

Earned value analysis provides a quick method to signal when projects are ahead, behind, or on schedule and over, under, or on budget. Just when those

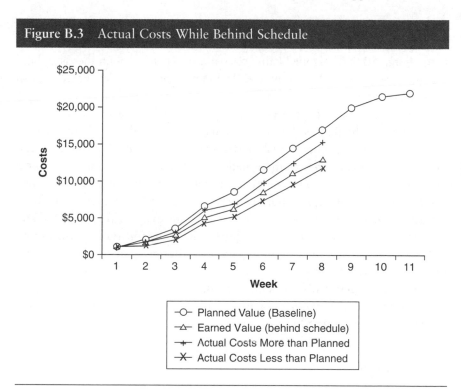

Figure B.3 Actual Costs While Behind Schedule

Legend:
- –O– Planned Value (Baseline)
- –△– Earned Value (behind schedule)
- –+– Actual Costs More than Planned
- –X– Actual Costs Less than Planned

"signals" become "red flags" and how to interpret and respond to them are managerial decisions.

CAVEATS

The managerial utility of earned value analysis must take into consideration a number of issues about the calculations themselves. First, the calculations are based on dollars spent. Dollars spent may or may not represent actual work done. Consider, for example, Dr. Howard's project in Chapter 4. Dr. Howard was putting together a rather high-tech laboratory for his research work on bio-informatics. Some tasks called for the installation of high-tech (and very costly) equipment. When that equipment is received, it can be charged against the planned costs of the installation task. If the equipment costs, say, $1 million, and labor to install costs $10,000 but will take a month to finish once begun, you can see an immediate problem. Earned value analysis could indicate that the task is more than 99% complete simply on the arrival of the equipment and payment of its bill. Rules of thumb are used to address what might be considered arbitrary and misleading calculations like this. One rule is to charge 50% of planned value once a task has begun; another is to hold off until the entire task is complete. The impact of such rules, however, can also be arbitrary and misleading.

Other problems in earned value analysis come from how people will try to manipulate the figures. Just when actual costs are calculated and charged to a project or just when a task is designated as "begun" or "ended" can make significant differences in earned value calculations. Project personnel are not the only people who might want to adjust the figures in earned value calculations. Client representatives may have agendas of their own (both positive or negative) that affect how earned value analyses are calculated and then shown to higher management in the client organization. Although all this seems to smack of dishonesty, honest differences in opinion can and often do occur.

These and other problems simply point out that there are limitations in what earned value analysis can and cannot do for project leaders. Like any management tool, earned value analysis has value when used with care.

ENDNOTE

1. Discussion of earned value analysis is limited here to schedule and cost variance.

Index

About the Author

Anthony T. (Terry) Cobb is an associate professor of management at Virginia Tech. Dr. Cobb received his master's degree in urban planning from Wayne State University in Michigan and his PhD in administration from the University of California at Irvine. Dr. Cobb first began project work for the Public Policy Research Organization during his PhD program and rose to the level of project manager. Dr. Cobb teaches a wide variety of management courses and integrates project management and team training into all of them. Dr. Cobb has worked for, consulted with, and trained personnel for a variety of organizations, making use of project management tools and skills and training others in their use.